Thrust in the Sickle and Reap

Earl Paulk

Unless otherwise noted, all scripture quotations in this book are from
The New King James Version.

Copyright 1986
K Dimension Publishers
Atlanta, Georgia

Printed in the United States of America
ISBN 0-917595-11-4

K **Dimension
Publishers**

P.O. Box 7300 • Atlanta, GA 30357

ACKNOWLEDGEMENTS

I wish to thank the Publications Department of Chapel Hill Harvester Church for their daily efforts and continuing dedication to the Lord in the preparation of this book.

I thank my Editorial Assistant, Tricia Weeks, for her capable direction in rewriting and editing these manuscripts.

I deeply appreciate the proficiency of our Editorial Staff—Gayle Blackwood, Chris Oborne and Gail Smith.

I thank Wes Bonner for his expertise in coordinating the technical aspects of publishing this book. I also give special thanks to Gail Smith and Donna Eubanks for typesetting.

Finally, I am especially grateful for those who give their time and skills to further the message of the Kingdom of God: Angela Hamrick, Linda Jacobson and Kae Rivenbark for transcribing; Janis McFarland and Jeannie Garthwaite for proofreading.

May the seeds of these words bear much fruit for the glory of the Kingdom of God.

DEDICATION

To those who are now, unknowingly, part of the great harvest of the earth; white unto harvest, waiting for the laborers, ready for reaping.

INTRODUCTION

As I have reviewed the final manuscript of this book, I cannot describe the anticipation I know in my spirit. God has repeatedly confirmed the message written on these pages as His direction for the Church in this hour. When the Lord directs His people, His messengers are always grateful for prompt, undeniable confirmation. I have reviewed this manuscript with much gratitude to the Lord and bold assurance of the urgency of this message for God's people.

I have spent the past two weeks in dialogue with some of the world's most renowned theologians and pastors from various denominations. The first week I was privileged to have been selected to participate as one of nine Pentecostals in the 1986 Catholic/Pentecostal Dialogue with nine distinguished representatives from the Vatican, meeting this year at a monastery near Fuller Theological Seminary in Pasadena, California. Though theological differences and misunderstandings historically exist, the Holy Spirit is leaping over walls thought previously to be invincible to bring about unity of Spirit among those who lift up the name of Jesus.

The following week I shared perspectives of ministry with a select group of pastors from some of the largest churches in the United States. Dr. Robert Schuller invited pastors of "super churches" from various denominations, based on congregations numbering between six and fifteen thousand members, to share vulnerable sessions of ministry exchange. The value of such meetings in gaining a broad perspective of where the "cloud of God" is moving across the earth today is obvious. The timing of these sessions from the perspective of my calling from God, and especially concerning the exhortation to believers reading this book, gives me great joy and confidence that I have obeyed the Lord!

The invisible must become the visible. Jesus became the visible from the invisible Word. From our present perspective, the reality of Jesus' prayer calling for a Kingdom "on earth, as it is in heaven" is invisible. "On earth" are the obvious circumstances of life, kingdoms which do not honor the Lord. But the invisible Kingdom of God must become visible in the Church. In fact, the Church is the Kingdom of God made manifest.

For the Church to become the earthly witness of the

realities of the heavenly Kingdom, certain things must happen. The Church must become a "single expression" of God's grace to the world. A "single expression" does not mean one organization or denomination. It does require that the Church in diversity become one in faith and practice of Christ's love.

To manifest "as it is in heaven" on earth, God's people must move from a "give me" attitude in their prayers to a bold "proclamation" of God's will. Our responsibility is to hear, do and proclaim the Father's will in authority and power. The psalmist wrote, "The Lord gave the Word; great was the company of those who proclaimed it . . . " (Psalm 68:11). To accomplish God's plan, prayer declares Kingdom authority on earth, "as it is in heaven."

The triumphant Church manifests a winning mentality. The Kingdom of God becomes reality on earth, moving from an "inward" vision to an "outward" demonstration through the power of the Holy Spirit. Winners never retreat in the heat of battle.

The true Church appreciates and cares for the earth as responsible stewards of creation. God loves the world, but hates world systems and forces which destroy the environment He created. Man's boundaries are confined to the earth. Man depends on the earth for life and sustenance, and he has been given the command by God to be the steward of this planet.

I know by the Holy Spirit that the earth is ripe for a great harvest. The time has come to pray like never before in history that the Lord of the harvest send forth laborers. Scattered sheep must enter into one sheepfold by the Spirit. When the world recognizes the Church as God's community of love by the demonstration of His life in our witness, then Jesus will come again as King of kings and Lord of lords to rule and reign upon the earth. Jesus would have never prayed that His body "may be one" (John 17) if the reality of that expression were impossible.

When Jesus returns, our mortal bodies will put on immortality. The earth will be purged of the corruptible and become new. The heavens will become new because heavenly forces in rebellion will be put down. And Jesus shall reign forever and ever. Indeed, the kingdoms of this world will become the Kingdom of our God and of His Christ.

Our King Cometh!

Earl Paulk

TABLE OF CONTENTS

*And I looked, and behold, a white cloud, and on the cloud sat One like the Son of Man, having on His head a golden crown, and in His hand a sharp sickle. And another angel came out of the temple, crying with a loud voice to Him who sat on the cloud, **"Thrust in Your sickle and reap, for the time has come for You to reap, for the harvest of the earth is ripe."** So He who sat on the cloud thrust in His sickle on the earth, and the earth was reaped.*

Then another angel came out of the temple which is in heaven, he also having a sharp sickle. And another angel came out from the altar, who had power over fire, and he cried with a loud cry to him who had the sharp sickle, saying, "Thrust in your sharp sickle and gather the clusters of the vine of the earth, for her grapes are fully ripe."

So the angel thrust his sickle into the earth and gathered the vine of the earth, and threw it into the great winepress of the wrath of God. And the winepress was trampled outside the city, and blood came out of the winepress, up to the horses' bridles, for one thousand six hundred furlongs. (Revelation 14:14-20)

1

CHAPTER ONE

The Revelation of Jesus Christ to John contained many continuous revelations. It began with a vision recorded in Chapter One and continued through the final chapters of the book, yet scenes of the triumphant, victorious Christ and His Church are recurring themes throughout the entire Revelation. The Apostle John restates his vision of Christ and conflicts in heaven and earth from several perspectives.

According to the Word of the Lord, angels have proclaimed messages from God to the earth at certain times in history. In the dispensation of God in these last days, an angel comes forth from heaven with a sickle proclaiming that the harvest of the earth is now ripe for reaping and judgment.

The time of harvesting the earth is imminent. Wheat and tares have grown together throughout the generations of the Church. Systems of this world can be defined as "tares." "Wheat," that is, believers who are preparing for the rule of Christ, are beginning to be a definable "people who were not a people" in the world today. God's judgment will fall as His people emerge as witnesses in the world. The time has come to test which systems will survive this mighty shaking—world systems or God's Kingdom.

Godless governments will view the true Church as an enemy and will make alliances with the harlot church and world systems. Confrontations between godless governments and God's authority, unlike any the Church has ever experienced before, will ignite around the world. Grave persecution of true believers is inevitable as judgment falls on the ungodly.

Righteous judgment begins in individuals, and the house of God must be purged before Jesus Christ returns. We commit our hearts either to world systems or to God's system, to mammon or to the Kingdom of God. John said, "Do not love the world or the things in the world. If anyone loves the world, the love of the Father is not in him" (I John 2:15). John was not referring to "the earth." He was referring to "the systems" of this world: kingdoms ruled by the lust of the flesh, the lust of the eyes and the pride of life. "And do not be conformed to this world, but be transformed by the renewing of your mind . . ." (Romans 12:2).

Elijah's confrontation with Baal worship on Mount

2

Carmel depicts two distinct systems engaged in spiritual conflict. Elijah, the prophet, stood alone with God. Four hundred prophets of Baal, a religion controlled by mammon, stood together in opposition to God's man. God's power is omnipotent. The god of mammon exerts power by using gold and silver to control society.

Personal sincerity is never a criterion for truth. Sincere mothers have fed their babies to crocodiles to appease pagan gods. People in cultist groups live in total sincerity concerning their beliefs. They sell flowers on street corners in the snow to support their cause. They walk up and down the streets all day spreading their gospel, handing out tracts. Sincere people knock on doors on Sunday afternoons, explaining their beliefs to anyone who will listen. They are certainly sincere, but according to God's Word, some are also very deceived.

The prophets of Baal were completely sincere in their beliefs. They cut their bodies as they cried out to their god. They truly believed Baal would respond with displays of divine intervention. But gods of gold and silver, gods of world systems, always fail in confrontations with the true God. After the prophets of Baal exhausted themselves trying to get their god to answer, Elijah spoke up. He prepared the altar, called upon the name of God, and God sent fire upon the altar.

Daniel was able to interpret the handwriting on King Belshazzar's wall (Daniel 5), and told the King that he was "weighed in the balances and found wanting." God weighs our works of righteousness, works which will establish His Kingdom, on His eternal scales. Our

3

works will be tried as by fire (I Corinthians 3:13). Faith is also weighed in the balances against other motivations in our lives.

Today God is "writing on the wall" that judgment is about to begin. He continually gives direction to His prophets. If we listen and obey, God will direct our families in experiencing abundant living. He will alert us whenever our children move out of His will for their lives. He will instruct us concerning the kinds of activities which will bless our families.

"Who shall not fear You, O Lord, and glorify Your name? For You alone are holy. For all nations shall come and worship before You, for Your judgments have been manifested." After these things I looked, and behold, the temple of the tabernacle of the testimony in heaven was opened. And out of the temple came the seven angels having the seven plagues, clothed in pure bright linen, and having their chests girded with golden bands. Then one of the four living creatures gave to the seven angels seven golden bowls full of the wrath of God who lives forever and ever. The temple was filled with smoke from the glory of God and from His power, and no one was able to enter the temple till the seven plagues of the seven angels were completed. (Revelation 15:4-8)

The temple was filled with smoke, the glory of God. Today something is taking place in the heavens as God closes His permissive will in certain areas where He once extended mercy and grace. Some people who have received God's grace repeatedly in their personal lives are now experiencing God's judgment, just as the nations of the earth are judged on a broader scale. God is allowing smoke to fill the temple. No interaction

4

exists between man and God except through intercession in the name of Jesus Christ. God is beginning to
interact with enough mature Christians who walk in
faith and obedience so that His judgment and reaping
of the harvest can begin.

> *Then I heard a loud voice from the temple saying to the
> seven angels, "Go and pour out the bowls of the wrath of
> God on the earth." So the first went and poured out his
> bowl upon the earth, and a foul and loathsome sore came
> upon the men who had the mark of the beast and those
> who worshiped his image. (Revelation 16:1,2)*

Who has the mark of the beast and worships his
image? The mark of the beast means intellectual
acceptance of world systems. The mark of the beast
controls the thought patterns of those who serve
mammon. They disregard spiritual headship. They
cannot specifically name anyone who is over them in
the Lord. They are married to world systems; therefore,
they eat and drink and are merry because tomorrow
they will die! That attitude indicates mammon's control! The first bowl of wrath poured out upon the earth
caused malignancy. Undoubtedly, we are living in a
day of severe malignancy affecting everyone with its
threat to life.

> *Then the second angel poured out his bowl on the sea, and
> it became blood as of a dead man; and every living crea-
> ture in the sea died. Then the third angel poured out his
> bowl on the rivers and springs of water, and they became
> blood. And I heard the angel of the waters saying: "You
> are righteous, O Lord, the One who is and who was and
> who is to be, because You have judged these things. For
> they have shed the blood of saints and prophets, and You*

*have given them blood to drink. For it is their just due."
And I heard another from the altar saying, "Even so, Lord
God Almighty, true and righteous are Your judgments."
Then the fourth angel poured out his bowl on the sun, and
power was given to him to scorch men with fire. And men
were scorched with great heat, and they blasphemed the
name of God who has power over these plagues; and they
did not repent and give Him glory. (Revelation 16:3-9)*

A national research team concluded that humanity
has abused the atmosphere. We have destroyed much
of the earth's protective covering. Today we see the
reality of "men being scorched" by the sun. Dermatol-
ogists encourage people to stay out of sunlight unless
they provide protective covering for their skin. Protective elements in the atmosphere have been destroyed,
creating problems in sustaining life on earth.

Scientists continually report that earth creatures are
dying due to pollution of the seas and air. The angel of
God allows destruction. Devastation through natural
disasters must increase until people make eternal decisions. (David F. Salisbury, "The Facts Behind the
Ozone Scare." *National Wildlife Federation,* Copyright 1975, March/April edition, pp. 33-35). (Nigel Sit-
well, "Our Trees Are Dying" *Science Digest,* Sept. 1984,
pp. 39-42). ("A Clean America, Will People Pay The
Price?" *U.S. News and World Report,* Feb. 7, 1977, pp.
44-52).

*Then the fifth angel poured out his bowl on the throne of
the beast, and his kingdom became full of darkness; and
they gnawed their tongues because of the pain. And they
blasphemed the God of heaven because of their pains and
their sores, and did not repent of their deeds. (Revelation*

16:10,11)

This "beast" is antichrist governments in the world. Darkness and confusion prevent any attempts to govern nations effectively. People are restless and rebellious. An example on a smaller scale is seen in certain industries which have so obviously been turned over to employees. Businesses lack any structure for implementation in meeting people's needs. Many times abusive employers oppress laborers, fostering hatred and rebellion against unjust authority. Employees strike to get their way, disregarding the necessity of order and headship. Those who have ears to hear, let them hear what the Spirit is saying! God ordained structure and justice. Anyone who refuses to understand His plan brings anarchy to a society, the workplace or the family unit.

The pain referred to in this passage is not necessarily physical pain. Because people are becoming disillusioned, they gnaw their tongues in blasphemy to the God of heaven. They refuse to repent, and instead continue to direct vile blasphemies at their only source of help. When will they awaken? When will husbands recognize that God has given them the spiritual responsibility for their households? Why didn't Sodom and Gomorrah repent? As the judgment of God is released upon the earth, all warnings to repent cease. The harvest is ripe. The time for righteous judgment of the earth has come. Amid chaos and confusion, the Church enters that time of reaping!

Then the sixth angel poured out his bowl on the great river Euphrates, and its water was dried up, so that the way of the kings from the east might be prepared. And I saw three unclean spirits like frogs coming out of the mouth of the dragon, out of the mouth of the beast, and out of the mouth of the false prophet. For they are spirits of demons, performing signs, which go out to the kings of the earth and of the whole world, to gather them to the battle of that great day of God Almighty. "Behold, I am coming as a thief. Blessed is he who watches, and keeps his garments, lest he walk naked and they see his shame." And they gathered them together to the place called in Hebrew, Armageddon. (Revelation 16:12-16)

The meaning of the sixth bowl requires an understanding of the Old Testament. When the Euphrates River dried up, eliminating Israel's natural boundary, Israel's enemies easily attacked her. This revelation is based on the same concept. The dried-up river indicates an opening for adverse forces to come against those who are estranged from God. Severe persecution directed toward the Church follows.

Satan subtly uses anti-Christian principles even in our government, such as zoning surveillances of God's Church. Agnostic bureaucracy often controls governments which harass churches without comprehending the spiritual forces pressing them to make certain decisions.

Charles Simpson reported that government representatives walked into his church and actually set up an office. The government closed a church associated with his on the West Coast. If we sit idly by and allow the government to regulate church affairs, America's religious freedom will soon become like Poland's or Russia's. What can we do? We must stand boldly for our beliefs; elect congressmen and senators who understand that government must never interfere in issues pertaining to worship in the house of God.

False prophets from anti-Christian religions deny Christ's incarnation in the world. "Antichrist" simply means "those who deny that Christ has come in the flesh." Good people are taken in by false religions through powerful deception. Anyone denying that Christ has come in the flesh, or the ongoing incarnation of Christ in the Church, has an antichrist spirit.

God draws lines' that no one can cross. "He who is often reproved, and hardens his neck, will suddenly be destroyed, and that without remedy" (Proverbs 29:1). Sowing and reaping are universal laws. God warns the nations of the earth, "I have told you how to govern people." Some governments oppress the needy. They press indigent people into hopeless situations. The rich get richer, while the poor get poorer. God must judge kingdoms that have not met His standards of justice and compassion for those in need.

Some believe that God possesses such mercy that His day of grace will never end. When God's grace is repeatedly rejected, the Spirit of God departs from people without their even realizing their day of reckoning has come. God turns stubborn, disobedient souls over to reprobation without hope of remedy. Someone in that state may even continue to preach and teach, but their anointing from God has departed.

"The Lord hardened Pharaoh's heart, and he would not let them go" (Exodus 10:27). Moses warned Pharaoh repeatedly, "These are God's people. Let them go."

9

But in spite of the horrible plagues that befell Pharaoh, he continued to hold the Israelites in bondage. Why? Pharaoh's heart was hardened by refusing to listen to God. He disregarded the prophet's voice. Instead, he said, "I am going to do things my own way."

Therefore I say to you, every sin and blasphemy will be forgiven men, but the blasphemy against the Spirit will not be forgiven men. Anyone who speaks a word against the Son of Man, it will be forgiven him; but whoever speaks against the Holy Spirit, it will not be forgiven him, either in this age or in the age to come. Either make the tree good and its fruit good, or else make the tree bad and its fruit bad; for a tree is known by its fruit. (Matthew 12:31-33)

The Pharisees accused Jesus of casting out demons by Beelzebub, the ruler of demons. Jesus called their accusations "blasphemy." Those religious leaders refused to allow the Holy Spirit to reveal Jesus' identity to them. No man can know Jesus except by the power of the Holy Spirit. People wear crosses as jewelry without knowing who Jesus is or the significance of the cross. Only the Spirit of God reveals Christ. Those refusing to listen to the Holy Spirit become reprobate in their hearts. They point at God's servants and blaspheme by saying, "They are evil." To accuse Jesus Christ of evil leaves no recourse for forgiveness. Blasphemy has no remedy throughout eternity.

Therefore God also gave them up to uncleanness, in the lusts of their hearts, to dishonor their bodies among themselves, who exchanged the truth of God for the lie, and worshiped and served the creature rather than the Creator, who is blessed forever. Amen. For this reason God

10

gave them up to vile passions. For even their women exchanged the natural use for what is against nature. Likewise also the men, leaving the natural use of the woman, burned in their lust for one another, men with men committing what is shameful, and receiving in themselves the penalty of their error which was due. And even as they did not like to retain God in their knowledge, God gave them over to a debased mind, to do those things which are not fitting . . . (Romans 1:24-28)

God says, "All right, you have crossed the line! Go ahead!" Judgment will surely follow acts of debauchery. Hardening our hearts, not listening to spiritual headship, not listening to the Word of God and blazing our own trails always lead to spiritual devastation.

If anyone sees his brother sinning a sin which does not lead to death, he will ask, and He will give him life for those who commit sin not leading to death. There is sin leading to death. I do not say that he should pray about that. All unrighteousness is sin, and there is sin not leading to death. (I John 5:16,17)

Some people continue to pray over situations which God has already declared reprobate. "Ephraim is joined to idols, let him alone" (Hosea 4:17). Systems of government in the world legalize acts which God judges damnable.

"Watch therefore, and pray always that you may be counted worthy to escape all these things that will come to pass, and to stand before the Son of Man" (Luke 21:36). Where is our escape? Various theologies and doctrines are contradictory. Teaching entered the Church almost two hundred years ago concerning "an escape" in the last days, a teaching which had never been taught as Christian doctrine before that time. The escape doctrine offered people hope of getting out of their conflicts. Jesus said, "I do not pray that You should take them out of the world, but that You should keep them from the evil one" (John 17:15). John wrote, ". . . He who is in you is greater than he who is in the world" (I John 4:4). Escape from worldly conflicts comes only through covenant with God. When plagues of darkness covered Egypt, God's people had light because they were in covenant.

Before Armageddon occurs, the Church must emerge so visibly that God can judge world systems by the standard which people witness within His Church. Every area of life must be restored by the Church to demonstrate the standards of God's judgment to the world. What is Armageddon?

The people of God were oppressed. They had little hope of winning a battle (Judges 5:8-19). God raised up a mighty leader, Deborah, who knew that God would deliver His people. The place where Israel fought the battle, called Midian, has the same root word as Armageddon. "Armageddon" signifies a place where man has done all he can do; therefore, God acts by divine intervention to bring victory.

Armageddon means "a place of confrontation." Many people believe Armageddon is a little valley near Palestine where godless Communist forces will one day confront the free world. The devil wants us to anticipate political and military clashes. A futuristic emphasis exempts Christians from assuming responsibility in spiritual confrontations today. Godlessness

12

is almost as prevalent in the free world as in Communist countries. Armageddon is not a historical war. Armageddon is a spirit. When the Church has done all she can do to call the world to repentance, Christ will literally return in the clouds of glory to judge the whole world.

The early Church understood God's intervention. They envisioned the final confrontations, the gathering of the enemy forces, Christ coming on a white horse with all His saints. God promises intervention against world systems and anti-Christian governments who have persecuted faithful people of God. All the earth will know the hour that harvest time is complete. The temple of heaven will open. Christ, who sits at the right hand of the Father, and all departed saints will return together to rule and reign with us on the earth.

A new heaven and a new earth will declare God's glory. The entire universe will undergo correction and restoration. The judgment of God applies not only to planet earth, but also to the heavenly realm of God. When Lucifer sinned in the heavenly realm, his fall took his angels to earth with him (Revelation 12:9). God's attempt to correct rebellion in the universe now focuses on the earth through His witness in the Church. But the conflict is a heavenly matter as well. Job was the focus of conflict in heaven. Just as God and Satan discussed Job's life, today God's Church is discussed continually in heaven where Christ rules and reigns.

Revelation 12:13 speaks of the birth of the "male Child," who is Jesus Christ. After Christ completed His mission as our Redeemer, He returned to His Father in heaven. The woman, initially depicted by natural Israel, enlarges her identity after the incarnation of Christ to encompass the spiritual Israel of God today, the Church of Jesus Christ.

Covenant means relationship with God, a relationship which feeds and cares for covenant people. In the wilderness, covenant people were sustained with manna from heaven. Their only protection from destruction was their covenant with God. Jesus even gave the authority to trample on serpents to His disciples (Luke 10:19). Satan has no authority over those who are in covenant with God.

Satan and his angels surround us. They control world systems. Satan is the god of mammon and false religions. Through the power of discernment, we can recognize satanic attacks and cast out demons through the power of God.

The New Covenant of the blood is activated by positive faith. Our actions are motivated and empowered according to God's Word. This covenant is lived out in consecration, dedication and commitment. "Therefore rejoice, O heavens, and you who dwell in them! Woe to the inhabitants of the earth and the sea! For the devil has come down to you, having great wrath, because he knows that he has a short time" (Revelation 12:12).

We live in the day of Satan's great wrath. The devil knows his time is short. He has infiltrated our lives through television, radio and other media. He subtly destroys youth with drugs, alcohol and immoral relationships. The devil is determined to destroy our

14

society. But God has a keen, sharp eye. He has a Church, men and women in covenant with Him who are right on the trail of the enemy, proclaiming, "Devil, you don't deceive us. Christ in us is the hope of glory! We are going to overcome you!"

The Word of God clearly indicates that Satan is bound. We overcome him by the blood of the Lamb, the word of our testimony, and loving not our lives unto death (Revelation 12:11). Satan sometimes appears to be stronger just before his defeat. Nevertheless, Satan and all of his angels are about to meet their destiny! The great white throne judgment, where God will judge mankind, will also mark the final resurrection for overcomers. Meanwhile, Satan is bound within the lives of believers, but not within the world. Jesus said, "Whatever you bind on earth will be bound in heaven, and whatever you loose on earth will be loosed in heaven" (Matthew 18:18). That promise is not a futuristic hope. Too often we permit Satan to control circumstances in our lives that we should never tolerate.

And I saw thrones, and they sat on them, and judgment was committed to them. And I saw the souls of those who had been beheaded for their witness to Jesus and for the word of God, who had not worshiped the beast or his image, and had not received his mark on their foreheads or on their hands. And they lived and reigned with Christ for a thousand years. (Revelation 20:4)

Some saints already rule with Christ in the heavenly temple today. The four-and-twenty elders in Revelation represent the saints who cry out before God to hasten His victorious rule and reign on the earth. The Bible says we are encompassed about by a heavenly host (Hebrews 12:1). They are on our side in the conflicts we fight with satanic forces.

> *But if I cast out demons by the Spirit of God, surely the kingdom of God has come upon you. Or else how can one enter a strong man's house and plunder his goods, unless he first binds the strong man? And then he will plunder his house. (Matthew 12:28,29)*

We dare not let the devil terrorize us. When Satan tempted Jesus, Jesus bound him with the Word of God. We also bind Satan by the Word. Satan may insist, "You can't do it!" But we simply reply, "It is written . . ."

"Then the seventy returned with joy, saying, 'Lord, even the demons are subject to us in Your name' " (Luke 10:17). Jesus gave power and authority over Satan to His disciples (Luke 9:1). Too many Christians don't even know their own identity in Christ! Some people talk about Satan being "alive and well" on planet earth. The devil is not well! He was wounded at Calvary. He has been defeated by Jesus Christ. The "late planet earth" will become a new earth, a place where Christ dwells in righteousness.

> *"Now my soul is troubled, and what shall I say? 'Father, save Me from this hour'? But for this purpose I came to this hour. Father, glorify Your name." Then a voice came from heaven, saying, "I have both glorified it and will glorify it again." Therefore the people who stood by and heard it said that it had thundered. Others said, "An angel has spoken to Him." Jesus answered and said, "This voice did not come because of Me, but for your sake. Now is the judgment of this world; now the ruler of this world will be cast out. And I, if I am lifted up from the earth, will draw all peoples to Myself." (John 12:27-32)*

Jesus promised His Church that even if we are arrested, He will tell us what to say to our accusers. If we are imprisoned before our course is finished, an earthquake can open the prison doors. How can we lose? We never lose when we abide in God's covenant.

"Having disarmed principalities and powers, He made a public spectacle of them, triumphing over them in it" (Colossians 2:15). Defeat is impossible for people who understand who Jesus Christ is and obey His voice. If we lose our natural lives, we see death as our transportation to the heavenly reign of Christ.

Now also many nations have gathered against you, who say, "Let her be defiled, and let our eye look upon Zion." But they do not know the thoughts of the Lord, nor do they understand His counsel; for He will gather them like sheaves to the threshing floor. "Arise and thresh, O daughter of Zion; for I will make your horn iron, and I will make your hooves bronze; you shall beat in pieces many peoples; I will consecrate their gain to the Lord, and their substance to the Lord of the whole earth." (Micah 4:11-13)

God opposes "mammon" or "Babylon," sometimes labeled "the harlot." People build bigger barns for themselves and never see the needs of their hurting neighbors. Many Christians' attitudes are the same as the rich fool's attitude. "I will pull down my barns and build greater, and there I will store all my crops and my goods" (Luke 12:18). People controlled by mammon see no need to invest in the Kingdom of God. They put their money into stocks and securities. Jesus uncovered the vanity of material possessions when He said, "You fool! This night your soul will be required of you; then whose will those things be which you have provided?" (Luke 12:20).

The god of mammon always emerges from the mind of reason. Those possessed by mammon have no ability to submit to God and never recognize the admonition of called apostles and prophets.

The Kingdom of God, the New Jerusalem from above, the bride, is a totally different system. People in this Kingdom sow and reap mercy, love and justice. They sow into the Kingdom of God and loosen the hands of the Spirit to work. They plant seed in good ground. They say, "Bless the feet that carry the gospel of the Kingdom. Thank you, God, for trusting me with wealth to invest in the Kingdom of God." These people understand covenant and follow the Lord without compromise. They know that God has called them to a higher dimension of life. They are **in** the world, but they are not **of** the world! They live in the world as a standard for God and refuse to bow to the gods of Babylon.

I give a word of prophecy: "The fiery furnace is imminent! Those in covenant with God who are thrown into the fire will discover a fourth man walking right beside them. And He is like unto the Son of God!"

Then I will sprinkle clean water on you, and you shall be clean; I will cleanse you from all your filthiness and from all your idols. I will give you a new heart and put a new spirit within you; I will take the heart of stone out of your flesh and give you a heart of flesh. I will put My Spirit within you and cause you to walk in My statutes, and you will keep My judgments and do them. Then you shall dwell in the land that I gave to your fathers; you shall be My people, and I will be your God. (Ezekiel 36:25-28)

This scripture describes "people who were not a people." The prophet was instructed to command life over dead bones. Today prophets speak over industry, the arts, drama, science, medicine, psychology . . . God is raising up an army ready to attack worldly kingdoms. He will knit ministries together as His Spirit empowers them, and together they will become a mighty army around the world.

> . . . and I will make them one nation in the land, on the mountains of Israel; and one king shall be king over them all; they shall no longer be two nations, nor shall they ever be divided into two kingdoms again. They shall not defile themselves anymore with their idols, nor with their detestable things, nor with any of their transgressions; but I will deliver them from all their dwelling places in which they have sinned, and will cleanse them. Then they shall be My people, and I will be their God. David My servant shall be king over them, and they shall all have one shepherd; they shall also walk in My judgments and observe My statutes, and do them. Then they shall dwell in the land that I have given to Jacob My servant . . . (Ezekiel 37:22-25)

Lifted to a spiritual dimension, this scripture refers to the whole earth. The Garden of Eden was initially God's place of correction, then the land of Israel, called Palestine. But now the whole earth is a recipient of God's grace. The tabernacle and temple were filled with God's presence. Heavenly places are filled with a great cloud of witnesses. And we, His temples on earth, are the habitation of God. As His habitation, we become instruments that God will use in correcting the earth. Let the reaping begin!

2

CHAPTER TWO

The generation of Spirit-filled Christians who reap the great harvest of the Lord in the last days will proclaim the gospel of Christ throughout the earth. A clear understanding of Christ's "gospel" is essential to those who reap this harvest.

I am convinced that misunderstanding has clouded the Church's comprehension of the gospel of Jesus Christ. For the most part, we have heard the gospel **about** Christ without hearing the gospel **of** Christ, that is, Jesus Christ's gospel. Both views are necessary for a Kingdom mentality. The gospel **about** Christ, Christ's identity, and the gospel **of** Christ, Christ's proclamation, are distinct and diverse.

The gospel **about** Christ deals with Jesus' role as the Messiah, Emmanuel, our Savior. His question to the disciples, "Who do men say that I am?" indicates Jesus' emphasis that people know Him as the promised one of scripture. At His baptism, the Spirit of God descended as a dove upon Jesus, and a voice from heaven proclaimed, "This is My beloved Son, in whom I am well pleased" (Matthew 3:17). Other familiar scriptures about Jesus' identity are: "For God so loved the world that He gave His only begotten Son . . ." (John 3:16). "And the Word became flesh and dwelt among us, and we beheld His glory, the glory as of the only begotten of the Father, full of grace and truth" (John 1:14).

> *And truly Jesus did many other signs in the presence of His disciples, which are not written in this book; but these are written that you may believe that **Jesus is the Christ, the Son of God**, and that believing you may have life in His name. (John 20:30,31)*

Jesus is both God and man. Bishop William Cannon, one of my seminary professors, taught that both the blood of man and the blood of God ran through the veins of Jesus. Jesus is God in the flesh, but He is also man. He is God to us, but He is man to God. God never knew the feelings of man until He became man in the person of Jesus. Because He was God in the flesh, Jesus demonstrated immutable, God-given powers: to heal, to save, to cast out devils, to perform miracles.

Through Jesus Christ in us, we, too, become sons and daughters of God who have certain inalienable rights in the Spirit. We can cry, "Abba, Father." We have access to God's throne.

For we do not have a High Priest who cannot sympathize with our weaknesses, but was in all points tempted as we are, yet without sin. Let us therefore come boldly to the throne of grace, that we may obtain mercy and find grace to help in time of need. (Hebrews 4:15,16)

Jesus is royalty, worthy to be praised and worshiped. We bow before Him because He is the King of kings and Lord of lords. Jesus' entry into Jerusalem was evidence of His kingship. People spread their garments on the road and worshiped Him as He rode triumphantly into town.

The character of Jesus reveals the godhead. "For in Him dwells all the fullness of the Godhead bodily . . ." (Colossians 2:9).

In no way do I minimize the essential significance of the gospel about Christ. I have preached it for over forty years. But the Holy Spirit began to reveal to me that the difference between the gospel **about** Jesus and the gospel **of** Jesus has misrepresented the Church's witness to the world.

Many people have been converted to Jesus Christ by verbally confessing that He is the Son of God, but unfortunately, some Christians have never been converted to demonstrating the Kingdom which Jesus proclaimed. That discrepancy in our message causes a tremendous weakness in the Church today. We know who Jesus is. We extol His deity, His royalty, His godship. But what was the message He gave to us? Why did He come? What was Christ's gospel?

Jesus Christ came to bring judgment and justice to

the world. He came that He might take over world governments! Those who believe in the separation of Church and state may cry, "Heresy!" Who decided that such a separation should exist? Many people have misinterpreted the scripture, "Render therefore to Caesar the things that are Caesar's, and to God the things that are God's" (Matthew 22:21). That scripture does not necessarily advocate a separation of Church and state; it simply reminds us of our obligation to government as well as to God.

The consequences of excluding God from government are obvious. We need only to observe the governments of the world today. Socioeconomic oppression is a hallmark of nations controlled by godless governments.

> *For unto us a Child is born, unto us a Son is given; and **the government will be upon His shoulder**. And His name will be called Wonderful, Counselor, Mighty God, Everlasting Father, Prince of Peace. Of the increase of His government and peace there will be no end, upon the throne of David and over His kingdom, to order it and establish it with judgment and justice from that time forward, even forever. The zeal of the Lord of hosts will perform this. (Isaiah 9:6,7)*

> *Now after Jesus was born in Bethlehem of Judea in the days of Herod the king, behold, wise men from the East came to Jerusalem, saying, "Where is He who has been born King of the Jews? For we have seen His star in the East and have come to worship Him." (Matthew 2:1,2)*

The wise men understood unquestionably that Jesus was born to be a king, one who has authority over government. Jesus did not come to rule as a king wearing a crown and carrying a scepter, the mere trappings of authority. He is the King who possesses true, godly authority, even assuming total authority over governments just as the prophet Isaiah foretold.

King Herod certainly knew who Jesus was.

*When Herod the king heard these things, he was troubled, and all Jerusalem with him. And when he had gathered all the chief priests and scribes of the people together, he inquired of them where the Christ was to be born. So they said to him, "In Bethlehem of Judea, for thus it is written by the prophet: 'But you, Bethlehem, in the land of Judah, are not the least among the rulers of Judah; for **out of you shall come a Ruler Who will shepherd My people Israel.**'" (Matthew 2:3-6)*

Herod did not fear Jesus as a popular preacher speaking from a pulpit. Herod feared that Jesus would replace him as a king. Kingdom rule is a vital aspect of Christ's gospel. He came not just to seek and save "sinners." He came to seek and save "that which was lost."

The ultimate rule of the earth will be Jesus Christ literally taking authority over godless governments. Admittedly, not all governments are godless. Many good governors, mayors and public officials witness to the presence of Christ within them. In a higher realm of dominion, Jesus came to dethrone Satan, the ruler over planet earth. The first Adam had lost dominion through disobedience. The second Adam, Jesus Christ, came to regain everything that had been lost.

Two aspects of our lives proclaim the gospel of Jesus Christ: being and doing. "Being" is important because Jesus **is** the Son of God, but "doing" is also essential.

Jesus said, "I **do** the will of My Father." "Being" is the first part of salvation in Christ, but "doing" the works of the Father is the gospel of Christ and His Kingdom.

That the God of our Lord Jesus Christ, the Father of glory, may give to you the spirit of wisdom and revelation in the knowledge of Him, the eyes of your understanding being enlightened; that you may know what is the hope of His calling, what are the riches of the glory of His inheritance in the saints, and what is the exceeding greatness of His power toward us who believe, according to the working of His mighty power which He worked in Christ when He raised Him from the dead and seated Him at His right hand in the heavenly places, far above principality and power and might and dominion, and every name that is named, not only in this age but also in that which is to come. And He put all things under His feet, and gave Him to be head over all things to the church, which is His body, the fullness of Him who fills all in all. (Ephesians 1:17-23)

Paul knew that Christ had rule over all powers and principalities. He declared that the Church was regaining the earth's control from Satan and returning it to Christ's authority (Ephesians 3:8-11; Colossians 1:13-18). The gospel of Christ proclaims that Jesus has preeminence in all things by taking authority away from Satan.

The Bible warns that a gospel of deception may be preached which might even cause some to turn away from the gospel of Christ. Paul wrote,

I marvel that you are turning away so soon from Him who called you in the grace of Christ, to a different gospel, which is not another; but there are some who trouble you and want to pervert the gospel of Christ. (Galatians 1:6,7)

26

We must discern the difference between the true gospel of Christ and a perverted gospel. The "other gospel" is almost a form of mysticism. It causes many people to live their lives thinking about something "way over there somewhere," never relating God's Kingdom to the "here and now." People fail to relate Christ's gospel to loving family relationships or responsibility for planet earth. Yet the Bible repeatedly tells us of God's tremendous concern for the earth He created. "The earth is the Lord's, and all its fullness" (Psalm 24:1). Revelation tells us that God will destroy the destroyer of the earth (Revelation 11:18). God Himself said, "I will heal their land" (II Chronicles 7:14). We are totally dependent upon the earth, yet we are destroying it by polluting the air, soil and water.

Christ's gospel is not widely preached from the pulpits of America today. Sadly, much of the gospel of Christ is being proclaimed by ecologists, sociologists and scientists who make us sensitive to the world that God loves. The time has come for Christians to realize the gospel of Christ is an application of His teachings to our lives and within our society.

Paul declared that people were hearing many gospels that were not the same gospel Jesus preached (II Corinthians 11:3,4). Many sermons preached today do not even relate to the central message of the Bible—dethroning Satan and reclaiming the earth for God. They do not relate at all to Jesus' message—the gospel of the Kingdom (Mark 1:14).

When God said, "This is My Son. Hear ye Him," He wanted us to hear the gospel of the Kingdom—

overthrowing Satan through Kingdom authority. Nobody disputes a message declaring Jesus as the Savior who delivers us from sin. But when we preach that Jesus the King wants to be Lord over every area of our lives—finances, time, relationships—suddenly people become indignant and tell us to stay out of their business. They say, "I want to be saved, but I'm not interested in changing my prejudices and my lifestyle."

If Jesus Christ spent forty days after His resurrection preaching the gospel of the Kingdom (Acts 1:3), it is incumbent upon us to preach that same gospel. The gospel about Christ is a glorious truth. However, without a demonstration of the full truth, we will never impact planet earth or regain Satan's domain. Christ's gospel was proclaimed by the prophets and planted in new churches by the apostles. They never even considered preaching anything else. The early Church did not waste its time singing about "cabins in gloryland in the sweet by and by." They addressed getting the devil off his throne and overcoming the powers of hell.

Paul declared, "I determine not to know anything among you except Jesus Christ and Him crucified," that is, the **power** of His resurrection (I Corinthians 2:2). Even in the closing years of his ministry, Paul continued to preach the Kingdom message (Acts 28:23-31). The theme of Paul's letters was that Jesus came to dethrone Satan. Of course, the Kingdom of God encompasses preaching Jesus' identity as its foundation because Jesus is the firstfruit of many brethren, the One who **personally** conquered the devil. But if our message ends with the identification of Jesus, the bride of Christ will never mature.

Those who believe that Satan is going to finally take over the earth and that believers are going to be "raptured" and leave the earth to the devil might just as well surrender the battle for the earth right now. The "good news," the gospel of the Kingdom, is that Satan no longer has any authority! He lost it when Jesus gave the keys of death, hell and the grave to His Church! The good news is that we can say, "By the power and authority of God, I adjure you, devil! You have no authority in my life!"

In the temple in Nazareth, Jesus read from the book of the prophet Isaiah:

> *The Spirit of the Lord is upon Me, because He has anointed Me to preach the gospel to the poor. He has sent Me to heal the brokenhearted, to preach deliverance to the captives and recovery of sight to the blind, to set at liberty those who are oppressed, to preach the acceptable year of the Lord. (Luke 4:18,19)*

Did Jesus preach the gospel to the poor to make them content in their poverty? Is it "good news" to tell poor people that they should be satisfied without shelter, clothing and food? A poverty mentality is not the "good news" message of God's Church! The good news of the Kingdom is that Jesus Christ is the way out of poverty; He is the Lord of finances. He not only owns the cattle on a thousand hills—He owns the hills as well!

Jesus did not come to say to the brokenhearted, "I'm so sorry you cry repeatedly over the suffering in your life." Anyone can say that! Prophets of doom focus on the problems of AIDS, Communism, pornography and abortion instead of the solutions. They quote statistics to prove the miserable condition of the world. The gospel of Christ provides solutions to problems!

Jesus didn't come to tell prisoners, "I see you're in jail. Be happy with the roaches! Get used to eating prison food! Learn how to live with a lack of privacy!" Too many preachers advocate complacency instead of contentment by trusting God as a deliverer in any trials or oppressive circumstances. The good news, the gospel, is that Jesus proclaimed, "You don't have to stay in jail any longer! If you begin to sing and praise God like Paul and Silas, this old jail can fall down around you. I will set you free from oppressive circumstances!" We don't have to remain captive in adverse circumstances for the rest of our lives! Jesus is the way out!

Jesus preached deliverance—He is the Deliverer. He did not say to the blind man, "Hello, good to see you! I'm sorry you're blind! You may never see a butterfly or a child's smile, but just hang on. You'll have a little cabin in the sky some day." Jesus said to blind Bartimaeus, "What do you want Me to do for you?" The blind man cried out to Him, "Rabboni, that I may receive my sight." Then Jesus said to him, "Go your way; your faith has made you well" (Mark 10:51,52). A message of restoration, deliverance, healing and hope is good news!

We need to proclaim the gospel of Christ to a world in desperate need of hearing "good news." Most politicians ignore the obvious fact that Nicaragua's political problems result from a godless government. Godless regimes control many countries in Latin America. My spirit grieves over a prevailing attitude among Americans that they should not be personally concerned about oppressive conditions in those countries. If oppressive spirits are not confronted by the Church in Nicaragua and other Latin America countries, they will terrorize the streets of the United States as well. Jesus came to set at liberty those who are oppressed. Liberty for all people in bondage is a universal concern of the Church. Bondage is expressed in many ways. Internal oppression binds one's spirit as much as godless governments.

Suicide among teenagers around the world has reached almost epidemic proportions. Many young people have simply lost hope. They perceive the world as a desolate place, full of sorrow, unbearable pressures and despair. One's personal attitude toward the future is one of the most influential areas in which Satan subtly operates to destroy lives. When Satan can distort someone's optimistic anticipation of the future, that person begins every day with an overwhelming sense of hopelessness and defeat.

The Beatitudes (Matthew 5:1-10) give characteristics of a Kingdom mentality, attitudes which confront negative thought patterns. Blessed people are humble. They know their dependence upon God. They are able to empathize and feel compassion in sharing heartaches with others. They also have great authority with God because they are meek in their own self-reliance, as Moses was. They are merciful toward their fellow man. Their hearts are pure, not critical or judgmental. This new mentality allows us to live out the good news of the Kingdom of God.

Instead of demonstrating a Kingdom mentality and lifestyle, even among Christians I encounter people who have given themselves over to mammon. They don't understand how to find fulfillment in relationships. They may possess everything materially, yet somehow they miss the greatest, most prized possession of life—fulfillment in God.

Jesus said that we win by losing. We gain the whole world if we give up the world. We gain everything if our spirits and our lifestyles please God. When we learn to give to the Kingdom of God, we always become receivers. The "least among us" becomes the "greatest." Humility before God leads to greatness in His Kingdom.

How can any Christian become "great" in God's plan? Jesus used two analogies to describe the methods by which we infiltrate the world: light and salt. The Kingdom of God is not established according to the principles of this world. We don't fight battles by manipulation, overpowering others, missiles and heavy artillery. Our power is the result of a continuous walk with God. Domination by light allows the world to see a fulfilled life, a loving attitude, good works that glorify our Father. Salt has a way of permeating any substance around it, just as a little salt affects the flavor of food.

The Holy Spirit empowers us to judge the ruler and authority of this world (John 16:7-11) and to reclaim "that which was lost" in the Garden. The Holy Spirit empowers us to confront godless governments and to become witnesses against worldly systems opposing God's plan for His earth. The Holy Spirit empowers us to continue the work that God has called His Church to do. The gospel of Christ is the authority of God, the power of God at work within us to restore the world to the knowledge of God.

I love to hear songs about Jesus. But even more, I love to hear the message of the gospel of Jesus: freedom, power over the oppressor, the ability to rise above circumstances, power to accomplish things for God in this present world, binding the strong man in intercession and plundering his house. The gospel of the Kingdom is all about authority to rule. That is the reason Jesus told us to pray, "Thy kingdom come, Thy will be done **on earth** . . .," in **this** family, in **this** hospital room, in **this** prison, in **this** governmental institution." "Thy kingdom come" makes an impact on the worlds of finance, art, politics, education, science . . .

God did not call for us to imitate or reflect the world. He called us to show His standards to the world. The world will worship Jesus when we act like Jesus, when we exhibit a lifestyle like Jesus, when we have that burning look in our eyes that says we have been with Him and move under His authority. We will have an impact on the way the world thinks and lives when we learn to demonstrate the gospel of Christ.

The gospel of Christ addresses three areas which define the proper function of the Church. **The first function of the Church is to bring people to wor-**

ship the true and living God and the incarnate Christ. God's Spirit is searching for people who will worship Him in spirit and in truth. Observing the Sabbath declares the lordship of Jesus, the sovereignty of God. By ceasing to labor as we do on the other six days of the week, we are saying, "Lord, You are in charge of my life. I don't have to work on this day because You are going to take care of me. You see the sparrow fall from the tree. You number the hairs of my head. I recognize You as the Lord of the Sabbath." In our worship on the Sabbath, the Church becomes a prototype of the Kingdom.

If people understood the principle of the Sabbath, nothing could keep them away from God's house whenever His people assemble. The Bible tells us that in the last days, people will stay away from the house of God. We are warned not to forsake the assembling of ourselves together (Hebrews 10:25). The Sabbath provides not only an opportunity to praise and worship the Lord, but also an opportunity to fellowship with one another, bless one another and allow the gifts of the Holy Spirit to flow through us.

The second function of the Church is to establish community. God is not pleased with Christians praying for "mansions in the sky." God is concerned with our witnessing through livable communities here on earth. God will supply every need of His house. But He instructed us to provide communities to meet people's needs—a refuge where people who are hurting can be helped.

The Church must address the establishment of

counter-cultural Christian communities based on biblical principles. The Church is not a sub-culture of
mammon—it is a counter-culture of world systems, an
alternative to worldly thinking. It must dare to address
issues and find solutions that the world is unwilling to
tackle.

I recently appeared on a television talk show where I
discussed one of my books. The host asked me about
our ministry to homosexuals at Chapel Hill Harvester
Church. In the course of our conversation, he asked me,
"Since AIDS is a threatening social disease, how do
you minister to these people?" Did Jesus restrict His
ministry only to those who were free from leprosy? Of
course not! How did He actually minister to lepers? He
touched them! He healed them! He was not afraid to
minister to people whom society had cast out!

I answered the question by saying that our church is
a community of love. If we were to post any signs on our
doors, they would say, "The whole need not a physi-
cian, but they that are sick. Come in and let us love you
back to health." Scriptures tell us that in the last days,
men's hearts will fail them for fear. Unless we truly
believe that the power of God is greater than anything
Satan attempts to do, many Christians will die from
fear also!

One day Jesus said, "You scribes and Pharisees, you
don't understand the gospel of the Kingdom. But the
harlots and publicans will listen to My message." That
same spirit blinds many Church leaders today. Gener-
ally, high-sounding theologians don't fully comprehend the Church's mission. The Church is not, per se,

an institution. It is an organization of strength. It is the life force of the Holy Spirit at work, God's community of love, God's Eucharist, God's sacrament in the world, leaven in society. When we understand the broad scope of the Church's mission, we throw our doors wide open to people who are sad, lonely, weary, sick, diseased, divorced—people whom everyone else has abandoned. We welcome them into the house of God where they will find healing, health and restoration.

The third function of the Church is as a witness of Kingdom principles to the world. The Kingdom is not a utopia, established by humanistic endeavors. The Kingdom is a reality. Christ in us is the hope of glory (Colossians 1:27). The witness Church is a standard by which God not only judges the world, but He also redeems the world.

If people opposing God's plan can't attack the message of the Kingdom, they attack His messenger. In the role of a prophetic witness to the world, the Church undergoes great attacks. Opposing spirits move to kill prophets and prophetic ministries. Modern-day prophets, such as Oral Roberts and the late Kathryn Kuhlman, have even been attacked by people who were once considered among those closest to them in ministry. Prophets such as Elijah, Jeremiah, John the Baptist and Stephen were attacked and even killed for speaking truths of God that the world found offensive or threatening.

Jesus Himself was killed because He was a prophet. When He acknowledged that He was a king, He prophetically announced His role and mission on earth.

Pilate asked Jesus, "Are you the King of the Jews?" Jesus replied, "You say rightly that I am a king. For this cause I was born, and for this cause I have come into the world, that I should bear witness to the truth" (John 18:37). The people said, "This man has come to take Caesar's place." The truth of the matter is, that is **exactly** why Jesus came into the world. He never denied it once. The governments of the world are destined to rest upon His shoulders.

A prophetic Church is either hated or heeded. No one remains indifferent to prophetic messages. As long as we say nothing about the god of mammon, we have no financial problems in ministry. But when we declare that people will either tithe or go to hell, some quickly close their ears and harden their hearts. They refuse to understand the uncompromising principle of covenant with God. Being in covenant with mammon demands nothing—selfish motivations establish that covenant. Being in covenant with God requires self-activation to please God, self-denial, observing the Sabbath, first-fruit giving, tithing, the Eucharist, forgiveness, unconditional love. We can never unconsciously be in covenant with God. Covenant requires a conscious decision of our wills.

The word "witness" comes from the same Greek root word as "martyr." The final overcoming power in Revelation was "loving not one's life unto death" (Revelation 12:11). Some even refused deliverance from death that they might obtain a better resurrection (Hebrews 11:35). Jesus Christ's gospel is not the "good news" of escape or leaving this world. It is not a gospel

37

of hiding our heads in the sand. It is a gospel of light and salt. It is a gospel of "being." It is a gospel of "doing." That is the **full** gospel—not just **about** Christ, but **of** Christ and **of** His Kingdom. Only the gospel **of** Christ will equip the Church to thrust in the sickle and reap the greatest harvest of souls the world has ever known.

3

CHAPTER THREE

When we began a church in Atlanta, Georgia, in 1960, God impressed us to name the ministry "Harvesters." At that time, all I had was a vision of what God could do through a ministry. Now I have no doubt that God has called Chapel Hill Harvester Church to participate in completing His work on earth. God is saying to His people around the world that the hour has come to thrust in the sickle and reap. Together we are His "people who were not a people" who are going to reap the earth in this generation.

I have proclaimed the expediency of reaping the harvest. I have warned that we should not sit idly waiting for Jesus to return. God's people have won victories, but unfortunately, at times we have failed to move forward in revelation. Often we fight the same battles repeatedly. The Church has been marching in place far too long. God has said to us, as a ministry as well as individually, "You have repeated the same steps too many times." The hour has come for mature, responsible demonstration of the Kingdom principles which Jesus taught. We must be able to identify our callings and be totally committed to God's work. As we are obedient to perform whatever orders God gives us, He presses us with further instructions. Obedience, action and forward motion are absolutely necessary to reap the harvest of the earth.

We must discern the times in which we live. Society lifts "weather prophets" to celebrity status. Jesus said of them, "You know how to discern the face of the sky, but you cannot discern the signs of the times" (Matthew 16:3).

God grants spiritual visibility to prophets to proclaim events and the relevance of those events to history from God's perspective. A prophet's words have no appeal to the flesh or the natural mind. Jesus said that man can discern the skies and say, "Here is the kind of weather we are going to have," but only spiritual ears hear and comprehend God's direction through His prophets concerning our day.

Spiritual discernment is our only means of comprehending and implementing the moves of God. The Bible is God's handbook to us, but daily enlightenment and understanding of the written Word come only by the power of the Holy Spirit.

Some people dabble in the arena of the prophetic word who have grasped only partial truth. Certain books which I disagree with theologically still contain elements of truth. Some criticisms, such as *Seduction of Christianity,* mix Napoleon Hill's teaching on mind control with biblical principles of how to use the mind of faith given by the Spirit of God. I do not quickly reject theories as being false because they sound "different." Truth is derived from many sources. The Holy Spirit weaves a move of God together from many directions and always confirms truth with "signs following" and lasting spiritual fruit. Spiritual direction and discernment enable God's people to understand the signs of the times and to distinguish counterfeit teaching from real insights into God's Word.

Recently I engaged in an interesting conversation at a convention with a television talk show host. I told him under what conditions I would appear on his program. I sensed in his spirit a deep desire to expose truth. He asked me to respond concerning accusations written against many ministers who hear from God today. My name was the last one listed before a certain author gave his concluding remarks. The writer probably knew the least about me, compared to many renowned ministers he criticized.

While I was still speaking with the interviewer, a woman who wrote a book about the dangers of the "rainbow" as a religious symbol stuck another book she had written under my nose. I looked into her eyes and thought, "Oh, God, I really feel sorry for this woman!" I perceived her deep sincerity and her strong desire for truth. She fights against the error of the teachings of the New Age movement, teachings which I totally agree with her to be counterfeit to Christianity. But she does not know how to discern the counterfeit from the real. Spiritual discernment comes only by the Holy Spirit.

We reap spiritual victories as overcomers from the world, the flesh and the devil. A number of scriptures refer to "the sins of the world, the flesh, and Satan." The devil sidetracks us with disagreements about methods and the time of reaping. We spend our energy debating theories of eschatology which are not even central to the message of the Bible. I want my ministry to help God's people concentrate on the central core of God's plan. We must understand His strategy for reaping and overcoming the world, the flesh and the devil. Failure to understand the issues and strategy in spiritual warfare leads to deception in our families, businesses, relationships and important decisions throughout life.

Jesus came to us as "God/man," living victoriously in an antagonistic environment. Immediately after Jesus' baptism and identification as the Son of God, He was led by the Spirit into a confrontation with Satan. Satan did not lead Jesus to the wilderness. Jesus was led into the wilderness by the Holy Spirit. The confrontation was between Satan and Jesus. Jesus did not fight Satan's cohorts—He fought Satan himself. His response to Satan on the mountain of temptation proved His power to overcome Satan's influence.

When Jesus withstood Satan on the mountain of

temptation, He confronted every bondage of worldly systems. John describes these bondages as "the lust of the flesh, the lust of the eyes and the pride of life" (I John 2:16). Jesus confronted and victoriously triumphed over all three areas. Satan tempted Jesus to turn stones into bread—lust of the flesh. He told Jesus to prove His identity by falling off the pinnacle of the temple—pride of life. He said that he would give Him dominion over all the kingdoms of the world—lust of the eyes. But Christ came to destroy the works of the devil (I John 3:8).

After Jesus confronted Satan, the devil left Him. Where did the devil go? He continued to confront Jesus throughout His ministry, and finally he came to us. How do we deal with him? The same way that Jesus did. We quote scripture to him. "It is written: man shall not live by bread alone . . ."; "You shall worship the Lord your God, and Him only you shall serve" (Matthew 4:4,10). We tell him that we are in covenant with God and that he has no right in our business and affairs. The devil has no new tactics. He is the same fellow, going repeatedly around the same old mountain, often deceiving the same spiritually ignorant people.

Jesus said that one sign of the last days is spiritual deception. Many will come saying, "I am the Christ. I know the answers." Without discernment of the Holy Spirit, this generation cannot fulfill God's plan to reap the harvest. Never before has the potential for utter destruction of the earth existed so indisputably. Never! Peter understood that in a day of great potential destruction, God would purge the earth by tremendous fires of revelation.

God's perception of "the world" must be differentiated from the way He views "world systems." "God so loved the world" (John 3:16). John understood the difference between God's love for the world and spiritual confrontation with world systems. "Do not love the world or the things in the world. If anyone loves the world, the love of the Father is not in him" (I John 2:15). Because of mixture in using these terms, many people do not understand the differences between God's love for "the world" and His hatred toward "world systems." We must comprehend the difference if we are to continue moving with God in fulfilling His will for the Church in these last days.

A scriptural understanding of "the flesh man" confronts the onslaught of humanism. Humanistic power originates through the mind of reason, which takes on the cloak of religion. Humanistic theology is tremendously deceptive. People who "figure out" the meaning of scripture by using charts, graphs and human reason become biblical humanists. They rely on human reason rather than the Holy Spirit's wisdom to bring enlightenment.

Jesus prayed that God would not take the Church out of the world, but that His Church would become powerful in confronting world systems (John 17). The only answer for confronting world systems and overcoming them is the mature Church speaking with one clear voice. We become God's extension in the world. We are not **of** the world just as Jesus was not **of** the world.

44

Humanistic religion is the opposite of "the meek inheriting the earth" by the authority and power of the Holy Spirit. The *Communist Manifesto* was written by Karl Marx, a self-centered religionist. Marx and Lenin rejected universal absolutes. They did not need God. They, as well as others, said, "We will pursue world domination." Recent political upheavals in Nicaragua, and those earlier in Korea and Cuba, have little to do with the people living there. Power-hungry revolutionaries aim at establishing a system of godless control.

Communism has so infiltrated American society that we hardly recognize its influence. The *Communist Manifesto* declares that Communism will eventually take over the world by humanistic beliefs. Humanism exalts human accomplishments. The government is god. When I speak of "the manifest sons of God," or "the Kingdom of God," I am not referring to humanistic goals or power. I do not believe that the world is gradually getting better and better by human ingenuity. World systems are growing worse and worse. But in the midst of chaos, God preserves an ark, a Garden, a people who are in covenant with Him.

Recently I shared in a presidential briefing of classified information at the White House. A young agent from Poland who works in the Defense Department and teaches at George Washington University participated in the briefing. His eyes burned with a heartfelt calling. He knows the reason he is alive. As he spoke, he captured his listeners with the urgency in his voice. He said, "You don't understand the danger our world faces today." He showed slides of Communist helicopters in Nicaragua. The helicopters, supposedly sent to the country to dust crops, are capable of launching rockets. Nicaragua is supplied with sophisticated weapons and tanks from Russia. As surely as Cuba and other places in Eastern Europe fell to Communism, Latin America faces Communist takeover.

Communists are not threatened by hearing Christians talk about "flying away" and "leaving the earth." A great asset to the Communist cause are Christians who believe, "We are going to leave the earth." The Communists admittedly want the earth for themselves. But the Bible says, "The meek shall inherit the earth."

My church was recently the topic of discussion at a Communist gathering in Bolivia. Some pastors from Latin America who have attended our pastors' conferences have been arrested in Nicaragua. They said to the police, "We are not going to yield. We have heard from God, and we are not afraid to tell you that you are wrong." During their interrogation, a Communist asked, "Where did you get that perspective?" They answered, "From an American preacher at Chapel Hill Harvester Church in Atlanta, Georgia." Let all the hell hogs of Communism hear what I am saying! The only answer to the spiritual perversion called "Communism" is the gospel of the Kingdom of God. God's Kingdom will overcome every power opposed to God in this world.

When a person decides to move from the kingdom of darkness to the Kingdom of Light, he puts on the armor of God. He begins to flow in Kingdom lifestyle, creativity and productivity. He discovers that God has an alternative solution for every system in the world that opposes God's plan. God has said, "Thrust in the sickle and reap." The Communists are also reaping. But God has said to His Church, "It is reaping time." Whenever one finds the Kingdom, he willingly sells everything else he has to invest in it.

Years ago as I started to enter a post office, two lean, gaunt-faced men who looked like they had anorexia stopped me and handed me a tract. The tract stated that the solutions to the world's problems were found in Communism. I started to go on inside the building when the Holy Spirit instructed me to go back. I spoke to the men, "Tell me about yourselves." They answered, "We are working in Atlanta for the Communist Party." I asked, "How do you get your materials printed?" With tears in their eyes, they answered, "We have been called to change the corruption of a capitalistic system. We use any money we make to print materials on our little printing press in our basement. We buy the paper and ink to print these tracts by eating only one meal a day. We are committed to giving out the gospel of Communism."

Too many Christians can't wait to sit down at the dinner table. We don't even consider sacrificing our appetites. When we have surplus, we occasionally say, "God, I am going to give you something." God says, "I don't want it!" God is looking for people who understand Jesus' words, "My food is to do the will of Him who sent Me . . ." (John 4:34).

We are created with the potential to become like

47

Christ. What did we lose in the Garden? What is to be restored? What is the full meaning of redemption? Not comprehending the answers to these questions leads to deception about the true purpose of the Church in the world. Many Eastern religions have bombarded American culture, totally deceiving people who are seeking meaning to life. We must remember that Satan transforms himself as an angel of light, not as a diabolical creature with horns and a forked tail. Satan's ambassadors fill pulpits around the world.

Moving from godly, spiritual direction to fleshly motivations is often so subtle that many people fail to realize whenever Satan moves in to influence their minds. Satan is totally deceived because he actually believes he is God. Many "ministers" perform paraspiritual activities, convinced that their ministries are of God when their power actually flows from the very heart and core of hell itself. Understanding the difference in ministries and having keen discernment of spiritual fruit protect us from deception.

God's judgment is not the same as accusations against Christians. Righteous judgment begins at the house of God, but Satan is an accuser of the brethren. Although certain philosophies in books written today contain elements of truth, the spirit of accusation within the text reveals Satan's influence. Warfare among believers in God's Church perpetuates disunity and confusion. Unity throughout the body of Christ can never become a reality amid such major conflicts among believers.

God's plan began in His heavenly estate, His eternal

Kingdom. God created a world to share fellowship with Him. Creation expresses God. I do not advocate a pantheistic theology which teaches that God is inseparable from His creation, but I do believe that God made the world to be an extension or expression of Himself. Everything that He created was "good." He placed beings of authority under Him with their own areas of responsibility. Michael, Gabriel and Lucifer were all extensions of God. God expressed Himself in these three personalities, but the archangel Lucifer rebelled. We know more about Lucifer, the fallen angel, because he is the one whom we encounter in personal, daily conflicts.

The Garden was not the first place of conflict. John the Revelator said, "War broke out in heaven," when Satan rebelled. That war continued on the earth in the Garden of Eden. We are also participants in that heavenly war.

And war broke out in heaven: Michael and his angels fought against the dragon; and the dragon and his angels fought, but they did not prevail, nor was a place found for them in heaven any longer. (Revelation 12:7-8)

The heavenly Kingdom no longer had a place in its structure for Satan and his army. In other words, when the Kingdom of God dispelled Lucifer, the fallen angel established his own kingdom on planet earth. The Bible calls Satan's kingdom "Babylon" or "mammon." Satan's kingdom is the "Jerusalem of the flesh" that killed the prophets, not the eternal New Jerusalem which descends from heaven.

Lucifer's dominion and authority are exerted primarily on the earth. However, in the story of Job, the Bible records that the sons of God came before God. Lucifer was among them. Apparently he is still granted limited access to the heavens. The Bible would never instruct us to "bind the strong man" unless Satan was a heavenly being, but he is no longer a part of the Kingdom of God.

Jesus taught that the Kingdom of God on earth began with a confrontation between spirits. His disciples returned to Him saying, "The spirits are subject to us." Their experiences of power over demons fulfilled the words of Jesus. "But if I cast out demons by the Spirit of God, surely the kingdom of God has come upon you" (Matthew 12:28). The seventy disciples returned rejoicing because they had cast out demons. Jesus answered them, "I saw Satan fall like lightning from heaven" (Luke 10:18).

> *How you are fallen from heaven, O Lucifer, son of the morning! How you are cut down to the ground, you who weakened the nations! For you have said in your heart: "I will ascend into heaven, I will exalt my throne above the stars of God; I will also sit on the mount of the congregation on the farthest sides of the north; I will ascend above the heights of the clouds, I will be like the Most High." Yet you shall be brought down to Sheol, to the lowest depths of the Pit. Those who see you will gaze at you, and consider you, saying: "Is this the man who made the earth tremble, who shook kingdoms, who made the world as a wilderness and destroyed its cities, who did not open the house of his prisoners?" (Isaiah 14:12-17)*

Overcoming power is given to the body of Christ on earth to confront satanic forces. Christ in us is able to confront demonic forces and cast them out. Victory over evil spirits is evidence that God grants authority and power to His Church. We expose deceptions even though Satan became the master of world systems (Revelation 12:9).

I recently met a man called by God to be an authority in economics who has written some outstanding books on that subject. I looked into his eyes and saw the intensity that God has been stirring in my own spirit. He was totally given to his calling from God. I saw a man who had been touched with the reality of God's Kingdom.

Economics is an area in which Christians are absolutely confused. Credit cards, which govern economic decisions even among Christians, create bondage. The devil is running our financial affairs. Covenant tithing and honoring God financially are tremendously important in showing the devil that we will not be subject to his control. Financial control is a central issue. Most people do not understand God's economics. They regard tithing as optional. Their actions indicate that God is not sovereign in their lives. Faithful tithing means, "Before anything else, I proclaim to the world, hell and the devil that God is sovereign in my affairs." Recognizing God's sovereignty is the purpose of covenant tithing. Tithing sows seed for a Kingdom harvest.

Man, redeemed by Jesus Christ, is God's answer to Satan's rebellion. No alternative plan for defeating the devil exists. God has not ordained another substitute to replace fallen Lucifer. God will win by our allegiance and obedience, for He has no other plan for restoring "that which was lost." Victory begins where we live: in homes where fathers are the spiritual heads of their families and wives are comparable helpmeets to spiritual husbands.

Ministry must be complete, "fitly joined together," to accomplish God's purposes. Missing God's plan for ministry destroys any hope or power for completing the task at hand. Ministries to singles, young families, women, youth or children should never become separate para-groups. They draw strength from the main thrust of God's ministry and witness. Removing them from the covering of a total church ministry accomplishes exactly the deception the devil needs to destroy lives. Leaving the covering of a discerning ministry insures defeat because proper eldership and counsel are missing.

God searches for people whom the Bible calls "a people who were not a people." God's "people who were not a people" become His extension in creation. They assume the place of worship and beauty that Lucifer once occupied. Lucifer also shared in the power of ruling with God. Our place must be one of taking dominion under subjection to God, as well as having authority from God. That place of authority is the calling of the Church in the world.

The Bible reveals how the "people who were not a people" are identified. The Bible is neither scientific nor sociological, although it contains elements and insights into both of those areas. The Bible is not a theoretical book. God's Word tells the story of finding "a people" who are restored to God so that they become His instruments of obedience. The Bible is the account of a plan of restoration. The world is engaged in a heavenly conflict because Lucifer and his angels control the systems of this world. God has placed His people in the midst of the conflict as a solution. The only solution to end this war is the incarnation of Christ, first as the Redeemer Himself, and secondly, as His body, the Church. The relationships of God to Abraham, God the Father to Christ the Son, and Jesus Christ to His Church are the three most important examples of oneness in understanding the mysteries of the Kingdom of God.

I omitted God's calling to Moses purposely. Moses served God's plan as a parenthesis by giving the Law. The Law served as "a schoolmaster," the Apostle Paul said, to bring us to a recognition of "right" and "wrong" and our need for grace and redemption. Therefore, the Law ultimately brings us to Christ, the Savior. Out of sin, the fall of man, the seed principle is established as the means of restoration (Genesis 3:15). The first evidence of obedience to God's voice was Abraham's answer to God. Out of Abraham's loins came the promised Seed, Jesus Christ (Galatians 3:16). Out of the loins of Christ, the promise of His Church was born.

If we fail to define the battle we wage on planet earth, then we can't possibly know how to fight. To accomplish our mission, we must say with Paul, "Therefore I run thus: not with uncertainty. Thus I fight: not as one who beats the air" (I Corinthians 9:26).

Finally, my brethren, be strong in the Lord and in the power of His might. Put on the whole armor of God, that you may be able to stand against the wiles of the devil. For we do not wrestle against flesh and blood, but against principalities, against powers, against the rulers of the darkness of this age, against spiritual hosts of wickedness in the heavenly places. (Ephesians 6:10-12)

I believe God is enraged when His ministers are preoccupied with nonsense, such as how they look. Vanity in ministry is an abomination to God. God said to me recently, "Vanity is the reason I put John the Baptist in stinking skins, out in the wilderness, eating insects." John asked, "Did you come out to see someone dressed in fair raiments?" The Spirit of God said to me, "Stop emphasizing outward apparel." God told the pastors in my church to wear clerical collars and vestments to confront religious prejudices and to become a bridge between Pentecostals and the liturgical high Church. If we do not walk carefully before God, we will even abuse that identification by emphasizing clothes instead of oneness in Christ. Personal loveliness consists of fulfilling God's purposes. Garments only help define and express a person's inner condition. We need to concern ourselves with putting on the armor of God instead of competing with worldly markets of fashion.

Do our thoughts in the morning focus on blow-drying our hair and caking cream on our faces? I am not criticizing wearing makeup or good grooming, but if we don't consciously put on the shield of faith, the breastplate of righteousness, and shoe our feet with peace and power, we will live a life of deception and futility.

Spiritual armor is absolutely essential in warring powers and principalities.

> *Therefore take up the whole armor of God, that you may be able to withstand in the evil day, and having done all, to stand. (Ephesians 6:13)*

Sometimes we depend upon counselors, convinced that they have some instantaneous psychological solution to solve all our problems. God knows that I have tremendous respect for the validity of academically trained counselors as part of our own ministry at Chapel Hill. However, sometimes worldly counsel is derived from satanic influences. Atheistic counselors who disdain God can lead the Church away from the true Counselor, Jesus Christ.

> *Then one was brought to Him who was demon-possessed, blind and mute; and He healed him, so that the blind and mute man both spoke and saw. And all the multitudes were amazed and said, "Could this be the Son of David?" (Matthew 12:22,23)*

People often regard spiritual counselors as mere men of the flesh expressing their opinions. They think with a "Nazareth mentality," saying, "I know his mama and daddy. I knew him when he used to nurse at his mother's breast." That perception of godly leadership disregards spiritual identification. Spiritual leaders walk in a new identity when God calls them, anoints them and gives them gifts for ministry. God calls ministers to a place of service to His people. The Bible exhorts us to ". . . recognize those who labor among you" (I Thessalonians 5:12). Understand the spiritual identification of those God has called into service in the five-fold ministry. Disrespect for called ministers of God places many people in a dangerous spiritual condition.

Many Christians have wanted to understand the meaning of "blasphemy of the Holy Spirit." Jesus said, "All sins will be forgiven . . . but he who blasphemes against the Holy Spirit never has forgiveness . . ." (Mark 3:28,29). Why? Blasphemy attributes the power of God to the power of Satan. Deliverance is a called and ordained ministry of God, yet some insist that Kingdom authority to cast out devils comes from the devil.

Blasphemers reject the only light that God gives them and turn aside from God's power. Some people who were enlightened leave churches because of rebellion in their hearts. Those people live in blasphemy and fail to recognize their fallen condition. People give hundreds of good reasons for changing churches, but if those reasons stem from rebellious spirits which resist the light and truth that God gives through anointed messengers, those people blaspheme God.

As the son of a Pentecostal pastor, I often "played church" as a child. When other children imitated speaking in unknown tongues, I refused, fearing that I might blaspheme the Holy Spirit. "Blasphemy against the Holy Spirit" actually assigns the works of God to Satan. Another blasphemous act is giving credibility to angels of darkness, religious "Jim Jones" types, by promoting their ministries as truth. Labeling false teachers as being "enlightened men of God" is always blasphemy. If we don't discern the truth, we can't possibly overcome the gods of this world.

The Bible says, "By their fruits you shall know them." I have no confidence in anyone who judges ministries, yet have no proven fruit of their own in the same areas of ministry they criticize. Are they caring for the sick and dying? Are they setting captives free from bondages? Are they ministering to people who have broken hearts? Do they have proven fruit of restored lives? Are they tearing down racial and cultural prejudices? Are they lifting up the name of Jesus Christ? Do they yield to the power of the Holy Spirit? Those criteria test our fruit and help us to discern truth. Fruit reveals God's power and blessings on a ministry.

Some ministries know how to use "charismatic terms," yet the heart of their message is deception. Privately they teach that "speaking in tongues is of the devil." Learn the difference between people who use "charismatic phrases," and those who are genuine in their hearts in moving by the power of the Holy Spirit. Some preachers insist, "I can do nothing without the Spirit of God," yet they have no understanding of who the Holy Spirit is and why He was sent to empower the Church.

As surely as prophets of God prophesy His Word, false prophets follow them with spirits of sorcery. False prophets may appear to have the same spirit as God's genuine prophets, and they will also prophesy. When prophecy comes to pass, false prophets claim credit for prophesying the event. Note carefully their other prophecies which fail to happen. Learn the difference between true and false prophets. False prophets do not function in some vast spiritual wasteland. Often they sit comfortably among people in Spirit-filled congregations. Learn to determine the source of prophetic utterances. False prophets are the source of many world conflicts at this time of harvest.

And Simon Peter answered and said, "You are the Christ, the Son of the living God." Jesus answered and said to him, "Blessed are you, Simon Bar-Jonah, for flesh and blood has not revealed this to you, but My Father who is in heaven. And I also say to you that you are Peter, and on this rock I will build My church, and the gates of Hades shall not prevail against it. And I will give you the keys of the kingdom of heaven, and whatever you bind on earth will be bound in heaven, and whatever you loose on earth will be loosed in heaven." (Matthew 16:16-19)

Peter's revelation reveals the meaning of the scripture, "Flesh and blood cannot inherit the kingdom of God" (I Corinthians 15:50). The Kingdom comes by revelation. Some people who quote "flesh and blood cannot inherit. . ." don't even understand the meaning of "flesh and blood" in this passage. This scripture means that natural minds of reason can never understand the Kingdom. Kingdom revelation does not come by "flesh and blood" reasoning. Revelation comes only by spiritual impartation from God.

Religion always seems to follow along behind the rest of society in a "defensive" role. God's people rarely set the pace or get to the "cutting edge" of world events. Religion stands around, waiting to see if political systems are going to affect and benefit society. After the damage is done, religion jumps on board and says, "We have something to say, too!" Christians usually wait too late before they take action or speak out on social issues.

The Church was the last voice to speak out on the civil rights issue. Church leaders ran in after the battle was finished, saying, "Me, too!" I refused to stand by while the battle raged. I was the pastor of a large church in Atlanta when the Lord spoke to my heart about taking a public stand on civil rights. Every face in my congregation was white. I stood up one Sunday and said, "I have heard from God. You can do with me whatever you want, but I promise you that I am going to take a stand for racial equality. We are not going to close Atlanta's schools because of integration. Black children in this city have as much right to attend public schools as your children do. I have traveled throughout this state. I have seen how black children are deprived, and I am going to expose the situation publicly. You do what you will, but I will do whatever God tells me to do!"

When I finished preaching, members of my congregation lined up to speak with me. Some of them said, "Don't you know the governor is not going to like us? Don't you know that we bake birthday cakes for him? Don't you know that we are his friends? Don't you understand that he is going to say, 'My God, what has happened to your preacher? Earl Paulk has turned into an integrationist!' "

I replied that I didn't care what the governor thought or called me. I only cared about God's opinion.

Today pastors readily claim that they fight prejudice in their congregations, but many times integration is really only "tokenism." Tokenism was born in the very pits of hell! Tokenism does not exist in God's true Church. We are either full citizens of the Kingdom or not at all!

> *Again I say to you that if two of you agree on earth concerning anything that they ask, it will be done for them by My Father in heaven. For where two or three are gathered together in My name, I am there in the midst of them. (Matthew 18:19,20)*

God wants Kingdom demonstration to begin in the family. If God finds a man and wife in covenant, He begins with agreement in that relationship. If God's people will listen and not miss what He is saying, together we will boldly challenge Satan's hold on the whole world.

> *To me, who am less than the least of all the saints, this grace was given, that I should preach among the Gentiles the unsearchable riches of Christ, and to make all people see what is the fellowship of the mystery, which from the beginning of the ages has been hidden in God who created all things through Jesus Christ; to the intent that now the manifold wisdom of God might be made known by the church to the principalities and powers in the heavenly places, according to the eternal purpose which He accomplished in Christ Jesus our Lord . . . (Ephesians 3:8-11)*

Many Christians do not comprehend the witness principle. God cannot judge greed in the world when greed abounds in the Church. He cannot judge a lack of love in the world when believers lack love toward one another. He cannot judge fleshly acts in the world when the Church cannot handle the flesh in Christian lifestyles. The witness principle is the heart and core of Kingdom demonstration. The Church becomes a light to the world through daily application of Jesus' teaching in our lifestyles.

Inasmuch then as the children have partaken of flesh and blood, He Himself likewise shared in the same, that through death He might destroy him who had the power of death, that is, the devil, and release those who through fear of death were all their lifetime subject to bondage. For indeed He does not give aid to angels, but He does give aid to the seed of Abraham. (Hebrews 2:14-16)

Through interaction between heaven and earth, God gives aid to His people. The heavenly host watches and shares events with us through observation and intercession (Hebrews 12:1).

The Holy Spirit is an advocate, giving help, comfort and power to the Church. The Holy Spirit did not come to make us feel excitement and jump up and down. God gave the Holy Spirit as a powerful Helper, our constant companion. We must understand God's purposes in sending the Holy Spirit to enable us to become His witnesses.

Christ's identity reveals the incarnation and the reasons God sent His Son into a chaotic world. Imagine the chaos of the entire universe if the devil were in charge! The universe would resemble the state of the earth now: governments at war; kingdom against kingdom; lust and greed motivating society. God placed the Garden of Eden on a hostile planet. God always works by plan, design and pattern. He called Abraham, the father of the faithful, in the midst of a hostile world. He sent Christ, His Seed, into a hostile social and religious society. He now says to the Church, "You are in a hostile world. Live out My ways as a standard, a witness, so that I can judge the world and correct rebellion throughout creation."

4

CHAPTER FOUR

Only three or four years ago, I vehemently opposed opening a private school at our church. I felt strongly that Christian youth needed to infiltrate and influence public education. Recently, however, the Lord opened my heart to the conviction that Christian parents are sacrificing a generation of boys and girls to humanistic influences in public schools. We must challenge this serious situation. One way we can influence the trend toward humanism is by providing an alternative school based on Kingdom principles. Examination of textbooks used in public schools reveal that religion is virtually an ignored subject in representing typical American life. Traditional family values are not presented as the norm, or even the ideal lifestyle.

Social Studies textbooks written for grades one through four define "the family" as "people you live with." The texts never once use the words "marriage," "husband" or "wife." Countless references made to "mothers" and other "women working outside the home" depict them in such occupations as medicine, transportation and politics. The mother "homemaker" is regarded as an unimportant role. Money, status and pleasure represent the major motivations for choosing an occupation. Family budget planning never includes allowances for the church or benevolences. References to the first Thanksgiving, the celebration of godly pilgrims seeking freedom to worship, do not indicate the reasons they were thankful. God is never mentioned. "Pilgrims" are defined as "people who make long trips." None of the texts include information about conservative Protestantism as a social factor of influence over the last one hundred years. The Scopes trial is mentioned only in relation to debates concerning evolution.

World History books on the sixth grade level give more information on the life of the Moslem founder, Mohammed, than on the life of Jesus Christ, the central figure of Christianity. Joan of Arc is included in the text only because she was a woman, not because she was martyred for her Christian convictions.

This alarming information was not the research of firebrand fundamentalists; it was reported by the U. S. Department of Education. They admitted their regret at being uninformed concerning textbook materials selected primarily by humanists. The curriculum was not monitored by our legislative branch of government; therefore, no checks and balances existed to provide safeguards for the content in materials from which our children are learning.

On prime time television the cost of "selling sin" is million of dollars per week. Christian ministers cannot buy prime time to broadcast religious services at any price. The Ten Commandments are profaned and ignored regularly in movies representing our society's values. Immoral activities are the norm; they are never portrayed as being sinful. Television's top rated "sinners" are idolized by millions of people. A February 1986 issue of *People Magazine* published the results of a poll concerning "sin." Joan Collins and her husband, Peter Holms, were featured in this article. Joan Collins listed activities she considers to be "sin." She is quoted as saying, "Homosexuality is fine within reason. Mercy killing of the terminally ill is justified . . . Premarital sex is perfectly normal . . ." She continued, "As a matter of fact, I would not want my daughters, ages 22, 20 and 13, to marry unless they have lived with a person at least for a year."

Murder, adultery, fornication and homosexuality are listed in God's Word as definite "sins." Ms. Collins and others like her have captured the eyes and ears of the public. We permit our young people to follow their examples in dress and behavior. Even Christian youth grow up imitating the glamour of people who thrive on materialistic living.

Such deception is described in Revelation.

So the great dragon was cast out, that serpent of old, called the Devil and Satan, who deceives the whole world; he was cast to the earth, and his angels were cast out with him. Then I heard a loud voice saying in heaven, "Now salvation, and strength, and the kingdom of our God, and the power of His Christ have come, for the accuser of our brethren, who accused them before our God day and night, has been cast down. And they overcame him by the blood of the Lamb and by the word of their testimony, and they did not love their lives to the death . . ." (Revelation 12:9-11)

How do the saints overcome? By recognizing the power of their covenant with God: salvation through the blood of the Lamb; their testimonies proclaimed without timidity in daily witnessing and covenant prayers; and not loving their lives—even when facing death, they will not compromise with the world.

Only Adam experienced creation in the full image of God. Except for Jesus Christ, all born after Adam were members of a fallen species. God said to Adam, "In the day that you sin, you are going to die." The part of Adam "created in the likeness of God" died. Apes represent the likeness of God as much as man does without the presence of the Spirit of God. The anatomy of an ape is certainly comparable to man's, but man is distinct among all other creatures. The Spirit of God within us enables us to make moral judgments in perfect harmony with God's will. That ability died in the Garden when man became a fallen species.

Only "born again" people represent the image of God on earth. People who are not born again belong to their father, the devil. Jesus said, "You are of your father the

devil, and the desires of your father you want to do . . ."
(John 8:44).

The image of God in us from creation is restored
through Jesus Christ's reconciliation and atonement
for sin. We possess the potential to reflect the image of
God. Only when we reach that potential can the Spirit
of God move in power through us.

We have come to understand the "world view" of the
Church's mission. The earth is the Lord's. World systems must be judged by what we call "the witness
principle." In the Old Testament, two or three witnesses were required to testify against those who had
sinned. The witness principle is consistent throughout
the Word of the Lord. Jesus sent out the apostles by
two's. The final witnesses described in Revelation are
two witnesses. God's Church is one witness, a standard—God's power of authority on planet earth. Jesus
Christ lived as "the firstfruit," overcoming witness.
Jesus and the Church are the two witnesses God requires to judge the world.

Two opposing forces operate in the world: the Kingdom of light and the kingdom of darkness, Christianity
versus humanism. God is sovereign in His Kingdom.
Satan is sovereign in the kingdom of darkness where
man becomes his own god, or the state assumes the
place of God as an ultimate authority. In Christianity,
God is the Creator. The kingdom of darkness teaches
that man evolved from some kind of lower life organ-
ism. Evolutionists theorize that humanity is the product of natural mutations. Christians believe that man
is made in the image of God. Humanistic philosophies

insist that man is growing toward an ideal by evolution, producing an eventual utopian state in which every man rules for himself.

Christianity has certain absolutes that govern life choices. Heaven and hell are absolutes. In humanistic philosophy, ethics of behavior are always relative or situational. Eternal worth hinges on vain hope, financial status and pride in human accomplishments.

Christianity proclaims God as our source of revelation. Revelation is our basis of authority—revelation which is recorded in the Bible, lived out in Jesus Christ, and revealed to God's prophets today by the Holy Spirit. Humanism contends that man is his own source of knowledge and wisdom. In the Garden of Eden, man chose the tree of the knowledge of good and evil. The mind of reason became his god. In Christianity, God is the final authority and judge. Humanistic philosophy rejects the idea of a final judgment. People supposedly evolve to some infinite, unknown state, unexplained and impossible to describe.

Humanists value people only as they relate to and serve the goals of government. The state becomes god to humanists because man is paramount. Individuals are considered important only as they relate to the state's needs and economy.

Regardless of their nationality, Christians are never inwardly ruled by oppressive forces, even under Marxism or Communism. Christians are governed by the Holy Spirit within them even in a totalitarian state where human choices become irrelevant.

Man is a spiritual being. Christians have the privilege of praying and touching the powers of God regardless of circumstances. We can fast and seek God, and God will divinely intervene in our behalf. Humanistic philosophy states that man originated through no more than a biological accident. To humanists, man has no eternal value and eternity does not exist.

God is omnipotent to the Christian. Dedicated believers embrace a covenant relationship with Him, giving their firstfruits to the Lord. Dedication to covenant says, "God, You are sovereign." Humanistic philosophy espouses mammon as the criterion for power. Debt or materialistic striving brings one under mammon's control.

Christians have the hope of a new heaven and a new earth wherein righteousness dwells. Humanists will never fully achieve their goals. Man is incapable of perfection apart from God. A utopian society will never exist in human history. Only total chaos and anarchy result from such a striving, competitive philosophy. World systems today resemble a utopia as much as humanists can ever hope to achieve.

The antidote to the rebellion of Lucifer is found in the book of Genesis. God said, "Let Us make man in Our image, according to Our likeness; let them have dominion over the fish of the sea, over the birds of the air, and over the cattle, over all the earth and over every creeping thing that creeps on the earth" (Genesis 1:26).

Man was created in God's image as a sovereign creature, able to make choices and decisions. Man's ability to choose is within the parameter of God's sovereignty, but God chose to give free will to man. Any person can decide for himself to become a Christian or a humanist. We become believers by choosing the tree of life which God has provided through Jesus Christ. After hearing the gospel, people choose either Christ or the power of reason by determining their direction according to their own minds and their own set of values. They become responsible for that choice throughout eternity.

I now rejoice in my sufferings for you, and fill up in my flesh what is lacking in the afflictions of Christ, for the sake of His body, which is the church, of which I became a minister according to the stewardship from God which was given to me for you, to fulfill the word of God, the mystery which has been hidden from ages and from generations, but now has been revealed to His saints. To them God willed to make known what are the riches of the glory of this mystery among the Gentiles: which is Christ in you, the hope of glory. (Colossians 1:24-27)

The Word "became flesh" as God's answer to human problems. **The incarnation of Christ, and His ongoing incarnation in His body on earth, became God's eternal solution to a chaotic world condition.** Jesus Christ is God's revelation of Himself in flesh. Mankind is very necessary to God's plan of restoration. We usually talk about man's "flesh" as being a negative influence. But committed to God, human experience and emotions are very important in demonstrating God's will. Choosing to follow one's flesh, one's own course apart from God's plan, always negates the power of God in our lives.

We become God's expression in the flesh by what I call "the ongoing incarnation" of Jesus Christ in the world. The Apostle Paul called the Church, "the body of Christ" (Colossians 1:18). John said, ". . . as He is, so are we in this world" (I John 4:17). We are co-laborers with Christ. We will be joint-heirs with Him in the ultimate reign of Christ on earth, but now we share His responsibility for proclaiming the gospel. Christ in us is the hope of glory. Jesus Christ is the firstfruit of the incarnation. We share in the ongoing incarnation of Christ, even to the point of sharing vicariously in His sufferings.

Some Christians give their lives prematurely or vicariously to cause others to recognize their spiritual condition or give them greater cause to press in Kingdom proclamation. I believe two people close to me who died recently, my sister, Joan, and Pastor John Garlington, were such saints. Someone may insist that they were merely victims of accidents or disease. I believe that some deaths transcend circumstances to become a vicarious offering to the Lord for the sake of His body, the Church.

Paul claimed to enter into the incarnation of Christ. Whatever Christ did not complete in His afflictions, Paul believed Christians would complete. Suffering for the gospel enters us into the vicariousness of Christ's suffering while we live in the world as His ongoing incarnation. Only people who are fully committed to God are able to make the claims of sharing Christ's suffering.

God has always spoken to His people through human vessels—prophets of old, Jesus Christ and the apostles and prophets of the Church. The Bible says, "The secret things belong to the Lord our God, but

those things which are revealed belong to us . . ."
(Deuteronomy 29:29). Humanists could never accept
prophetic teaching. Spiritual revelation is considered
to be "foolishness" to them. "Surely the Lord God does
nothing unless He reveals His secret to His servants
the prophets" (Amos 3:7). God expresses Himself by the
power of revelation to His incarnation in flesh today,
the Church in the world.

Spiritual authority cannot be separated from revelation from God. God uses revelation to bring us to the
knowledge of His will. Through Holy Spirit revelation
based on the foundation of God's written Word, we are
able to share with God in the process of recovering the
earth. Restoration and recovery are goals of God's witnesses who are empowered by His Spirit. Their witness
fills the earth with His glory.

> *These things I have spoken to you, that you should not be
> made to stumble. They will put you out of the synagogues;
> yes, the time is coming that whoever kills you will think
> that he offers God service. And these things they will do to
> you because they have not known the Father nor Me. But
> these things I have told you, that when the time comes,
> you may remember that I told you of them. And these
> things I did not say to you at the beginning, because I was
> with you. But now I go away to Him who sent Me, and
> none of you asks Me, "Where are You going?" But because
> I have said these things to you, sorrow has filled your
> heart. (John 16:1-6)*

We are living in the day when people will kill and
imprison true Christians, and even claim that they are
doing service to God. Many people in secular, humanistic institutions think the most noble act they can com-

mit is killing prophets and preachers of the gospel of the Kingdom. The first command of the Communist regime in Nicaragua was to silence Christian pastors. They think they are doing mankind a service because their god is the state. F. Houtart and E. Pin, noted Liberation theologians, wrote in *The Church and the Latin American Revolution,* "Latin America can no longer afford the time for evolution. There is only one choice: Revolution, that is, radical transformation of some kind or other" (New York, 1965; p. 256).

Nevertheless I tell you the truth. It is to your advantage that I go away; for if I do not go away, the Helper will not come to you; but if I depart, I will send Him to you. And when He has come, He will convict the world of sin, and of righteousness, and of judgment: of sin, because they do not believe in Me; of righteousness, because I go to My Father and you see Me no more; of judgment, because the ruler of this world is judged. I still have many things to say to you, but you cannot bear them now. However, when He, the Spirit of truth, has come, He will guide you into all truth; for He will not speak on His own authority, but whatever He hears He will speak; and He will tell you things to come. He will glorify Me, for He will take of what is Mine and declare it to you. All things that the Father has are Mine. Therefore I said that He will take of Mine and declare it to you. (John 16:7-15)

Christ was one person, limited to ministry in only one place at a time. In order to minister as an omnipresent Spirit, Jesus relinquished His fleshly dimension with its limitations of time and place. He entered a higher realm of restoration and love by becoming an indwelling Spirit.

"When He, the Spirit of truth, has come, He will guide

you into all truth . . ." (John 16:13). Fresh revelation is necessary to guide us into all truth. Had "all truth" been given to us already, Jesus would have never said that the Holy Spirit would serve as "a guide" to us. The Holy Spirit never leads us to teaching that diminishes, negates or contradicts the revealed Word of God. The Word is only illuminated to a greater dimension by revelation of the Holy Spirit.

God said to Daniel, "Go your way, Daniel, for the words [Daniel's revelation] are closed up and sealed till the time of the end" (Daniel 12:9). While the Bible is the basis of truth, God yet speaks direction to prophets and apostles in every generation. God's prophetic Word is given to evangelists, pastors and teachers who break down the revelation for masses of people to comprehend and apply to their lives. Not only is revelation always judged by the standard of the Word of God, but also it must be consistent with the life and character of Jesus Christ.

Paul said that the apostle, prophet, evangelist, pastor and teacher were given to the Church ". . . for the equipping of the saints for the work of ministry, for the edifying of the body of Christ, till we all come to the unity of the faith and the knowledge of the son of God, to a perfect man, to the measure of the stature of the fullness of Christ . . ." (Ephesians 4:11-13).

What is the role of the Holy Spirit in the world today? He receives direction from the Father and declares the works of Christ to people with open hearts who are seeking God's will. Someone may say, "I thought the purpose of receiving the Holy Spirit was to speak in tongues." No, the Holy Spirit intercedes for us, beyond our natural minds, to communicate directly with God.

The Holy Spirit enables us to become witnesses of Jesus Christ. The Charismatic Movement, as most people perceive it, has greatly misrepresented the purposes of receiving the Holy Spirit. Although joyful exuberance of the baptism of the Holy Spirit filled a great void in the Church, for many people the Charismatic Movement focused on an emotional expression of personal joy and fulfillment rather than the expression of God's heart—to confront world systems through His power. Rejecting revelation through God's prophets prevented the maturing of the Church; therefore, believers remained weak and ineffective in their witness.

The disciples asked Jesus, "Lord, will You at this time restore the kingdom to Israel?" (Acts 1:6). Jesus' response indicates, "You don't need to worry about that! You shall receive power and authority after the Holy Spirit has come upon you." Our fleshly bodies become the dwelling place of the Holy Spirit as we dedicate ourselves to the Lord. Why? So we may become powerful witnesses, confronting worldly systems.

People often ask whether a salvation experience qualifies Christians adequately to live as true witnesses. The Holy Spirit is essential in enabling us to be involved in the recovery of the earth, to enter combat in spiritual struggles and to live victoriously. We can only be witnesses by an act of our wills as we yield to the Holy Spirit. Christians will never reach their full potential spiritually until they release their wills to God.

God has given two areas of ministry to the Church: gifts and callings. Gifts of the Holy Spirit are listed in I Corinthians 12. Callings are listed in Ephesians 4:11. Apostles, prophets, evangelists, pastors and teachers are callings of God which serve as gifts to the body of Christ in performing their ministry. The gifts of the spirit and the gifts of ministries enable us to move under God's direction in the world. We live daily as expressions of God, men and women empowered by the Holy Spirit.

God has spoken to His people saying, "I want you to know your value. I want you to know your potential power and authority." A prostitution of positive believing often becomes a pseudo-religion. Some teaching on "self-esteem" and "success in life" become a para-teaching, distracting God's people from the main thrust of revelation to the body of Christ. But other teachings, such as those emphasizing our "worth" in God's will, are both valuable and valid. We must discern teaching, separating "the precious" from "the worthless" according to scriptural principles.

Today many preach that regeneration through Jesus Christ is not necessary to one's seeking to improve his self-esteem. Classes and seminars are conducted on topics such as "How to Build Yourself Up" and "How To Be Successful." Such goals apart from redemption and godly motivations are purely humanistic. Health spas are basically humanistic clubs for self-aggrandizement. People with humanistic spirits jog at the park on Sundays, while the body of Christ worships. If questioned about their motivations, the joggers will answer, "I am improving my health and self-image."

Many people cannot maintain weight loss because they continuously try silly diets. After awhile, not only will they remain just as overweight as they ever were, they will gain even more weight. Until we are able to discipline our appetites by bringing ourselves spiritually under God's control, we will never overcome self-indulgence. We must learn the difference between humanistic thinking and spiritual enlightenment in becoming the best that we can be to glorify God.

Many follow nutritional fads which have nothing to do with spiritual discipline. Self-improvement programs will bring neither lasting results nor significant inner satisfaction. Of course, we should not overeat. Broiled fish, chicken and plenty of vegetables are a healthy, basic diet. But weight control must never become a dominating obsession which focuses our thoughts on vanity.

The granddaddy of positive thinking and humanism, Napoleon Hill, reveals in his writings that he did not espouse a Christian perspective except as a limited influence. Much of his teaching sounds initially like Christian discipline of our thoughts, but the motivations of such discipline do not honor the Lord. The Apostle Paul said, "Finally, brethren, whatever things are true, whatever things are noble, whatever things are just, whaever things are pure, whatever things are lovely, whatever things are of good report, if there is any virtue and if there is anything praiseworthy—meditate on these things" (Philippians

4:8). The Bible tells us that as a man ". . . thinks in his heart, so is he" (Proverbs 23:7). But when a desire for success and wealth dominate one's thinking, the motivations are humanistic rather than motivated by the Holy Spirit.

One aspect of the teaching of the New Age Movement advocates meditation, yoga and strict nutrition to improve oneself. The goal is to project a beautiful image. Some men would allow their wives to go hungry, if necessary, to have money to pay their dues at the spa. Many people are distracted from the important issues of life with physical and intellectual vanity. Self-improvement becomes their main focus. They would never even consider skipping meals to help someone in need, but they regularly skip meals doing aerobics to maintain an ideal weight. That motivation is humanistic, totally disregarding the physical body as a temple of the Holy Spirit. The dominant motivation stems from selfishness, a "self" worship.

People suffering from anorexia nervosa have distorted views of themselves. They perceive themselves as obese when they actually look like skeletons. Even medical weight charts can be deceptive. We should weigh whatever God approves as proper and right for us. We should never permit worldly standards of beauty to decide our proper weight. When we feel strong, think pure thoughts and are confident of our appearance, we are also pleasing to God.

Jesus said, "My Kingdom is not of this world" (John 18:36). He didn't mean that His Kingdom was not on this earth; He was speaking of world systems. The

Kingdom will never come by human will, stringent discipline, guns or terrorism. The Kingdom will be established only by the Spirit of God moving through human flesh. ". . . Not by might, nor by power, but by My Spirit, says the Lord of hosts" (Zechariah 4:6).

What is our final hope in the flesh? Jesus Christ personified the hope of heaven lived out upon the earth. The glorious hope is not in our human accomplishments or efforts. Our accomplishments rest in what God has called us to be, moving with God's authority and the power of the Holy Spirit. The culmination of all things will be Christ's return. By divine intervention, He will overthrow opposing powers that are yet to be conquered on planet earth. We will have finished our mission as living witnesses through confrontations with world systems. But the "mop up action," the final victory, will come through Christ Himself.

For the grace of God that brings salvation has appeared to all men, teaching us that, denying ungodliness and worldly lusts, we should live soberly, righteously, and godly in the present age, looking for the blessed hope and glorious appearing of our great God and Savior Jesus Christ, who gave Himself for us, that He might redeem us from every lawless deed and purify for Himself His own special people, zealous for good works. Speak these things, exhort, and rebuke with all authority. Let no one despise you. (Titus 2:11-15)

Christ must have a Church which represents truth. A standard, a universal witness precedes Christ's return to judge the world. Then He can say, "I had a standard in the world for you to follow, but you refused it."

Because of our size and visibility, some people refer to

Chapel Hill Harvester Church in Atlanta as one of the "super churches" in America. I am often invited to sit with pastors of other "super churches" in sessions to discuss our spiritual victories and concerns in ministry. I am invited because the membership at Chapel Hill Harvester Church is an unusual group. Most churches in America average less than one hundred people attending regularly on Sundays. I read recently that of the 250 to 300 million people in our nation, only about 30 million attend church on a regular basis. And yet we claim that America is a Christian nation!

Christian commitment reflects our understanding of covenant with God. When we started preaching about God's covenant symbol, the rainbow, the New Age Movement publicly identified the rainbow as their own symbol. We refused to back away from God's Word. We said, "The rainbow is God's idea! We will not allow people teaching a counterfeit gospel to take the rainbow as a symbol of covenant away from us!"

Satan has subtly deceived minds, causing Christians to disregard their responsibilities. A utopian attitude or post-tribulation mentality breeds deception. Responsible Christianity, a concept of the world situation and our task of restoring "that which was lost," is necessary to perform God's will.

What was the response of people in Latin America, North Korea and Eastern Europe when enemy forces invaded? Many people kept quiet. We must examine our commitment even before the battle accelerates. Would we really give our lives to defend our beliefs? Would we go along with the crowd to avoid conflict?

Would we compromise our convictions to save ourselves? God is searching for a people who are so absolutely dedicated to Jesus and His Kingdom that they would willingly give their lives. That degree of obedience is the final test. Today Latin Americans who embrace the Kingdom message are in the thralls of such testings.

Political upheavals threaten American social order in the near future. Only by the supernatural power of the Holy Spirit through prayer and fasting will God's mission be accomplished. Prayer must never become self-centered. Our intentions parallel God's intentions in true Kingdom service. Prayer, at its best, always submits our wills to God's will. I cannot overemphasize the power of prayer in our lives. Prayer is an attitude of a penitent heart, forgiven by God, walking before God circumspectly, knowing God's forgiveness fully as the result of forgiving others.

Only those comprehending the grace of God in their hearts become instruments to dispense the grace of God to the world. Churches must become cities of refuge to their communities. They must accept the responsibility to reach out and lift up hurting people. Only then do we demonstrate the incarnation of God in the world. Prayer power, the gift ministries and the gift of the Holy Spirit enable God's Church to fulfill His promises upon the earth.

5

CHAPTER FIVE

Christians engaged in Kingdom warfare need to know the opposition's tactics. In any kind of conflict, the best defensive techniques are derived from understanding the enemy's offensive moves. A good coach prepares his team to move against the opposing team's strategy. A winning team plays both a good defense and a good offense. Undoubtedly, Satan realizes his time is short. He will move with great force across the earth as harvest time approaches.

To equip His army, God's Word gives detailed information about Satan's strategy. Old Testament accounts of God's interaction with Israel give understanding of the character of God. The New Testament teaches how

"God in us" confronts Satan. The experiences in the Garden of Eden reveal the character of God as Creator. God wanted fellowship. Therefore, He made Himself vulnerable to His creation. He gave them the option of obedience or disobedience, the tree of the knowledge of good and evil or the tree of life. We are also given accounts in God's Word of Satan's nature and his cunning devices.

Satan's power was another force in the Garden. His persuasive temptations deceived Adam and Eve. Satan appeals to the mind of reason. He promised, "You will be like God . . ." Satan said to Eve, "You don't have to listen to authority. You are also an authority, a god unto yourself." Satan is subtle and deceptive, but he clothes himself with appealing beauty.

The book of Esther gives insights into spiritual warfare. This story depicts confrontations between kingdoms and many analogies can be drawn from this account of Jewish history. The king represents governmental and political powers. Vashti, the wife of the king, represents religious systems. Religious systems are self-serving. Vashti rebelled against authority by refusing the invitation to the King's banquet, insisting instead upon having her own party with the women (Esther 1:9).

Esther depicts the true Church. Her story illustrates confrontation between world systems and God's Kingdom. Haman represents Satan. Haman's goal was to kill the Jews, God's people. Esther's obedience to Mordecai, who portrays the Holy Spirit, meant risking her own life. Will the Church follow the spirit of Vashti who exerts her own authority, or the spirit of Esther who moved in obedience to God's voice?

Daniel is also a story of world confrontations. Daniel, Shadrach, Meshach and Abednego lived by a totally different standard than their Babylonian captors. They witnessed for God through their lifestyles. They even ate differently. Finally the conflicting systems met in a head-on collision. Daniel refused to allow the government to dictate to him whether or not he could pray to his God.

Most Christians say that they would never bow to the gods of this world. No? Let's examine our lifestyles! Who determines the way we live? Who determines the kinds of houses we purchase? Who determines the neighborhoods where we choose to live? We need to ask, "What are our values? How do we spend our money? How do we spend our time? What are our conflicts? What are the confrontations we face?"

". . . in the last days perilous times will come: for men will be lovers of themselves, lovers of money, boasters, proud, blasphemers, disobedient to parents, unthankful, unholy . . ." (II Timothy 3:1,2). That passage foretells kingdom against kingdom confrontation. Within each Christian, two kingdoms clash in warfare: the kingdom of self-will or self-design, and the Kingdom of God which is obedience in following the voice of the Spirit.

Kingdom warfare begins as an internal battle. All of us initially resist God's plan for our lives until we realize our own inadequacies. True disciples finally bow humbly before God's will for their lives. Through the power of the Holy Spirit, we can say, "God, I submit my kingdom to Your Kingdom. I refuse to bow to the influence of the kingdoms of this world. I bow to the Kingdom of God in complete and total obedience." Covenant with God means total obedience to Him. In the midst of great warfare, we are challenged to enter into covenant living today like never before in the Christian Church.

The Book of Exodus records conflicts between two systems. Moses and the children of Israel challenged the system represented by Pharaoh's Egyptian government. Moses served as a spokesman for God who simply identified Himself as, "I am that I am." Pharaoh represented the gods of animals, the sun, the river and earth creatures. The plagues that God imposed upon Egypt were plagues relating to the Egyptian gods, bringing about confrontation between two systems of worship.

Today God is also confronting the gods of this world—the god of reason, aggressiveness, lawlessness, finance, socioeconomic systems . . . Humanistic religious systems confront the church on a world-wide scale. Central and South America are experiencing conflict between godless Communism and the system of free enterprise which allows men the freedom to live out their God-given rights and opportunities.

Exodus gives an account of the Hebrews going to Egypt as a solution to famine. I believe that famine existed because of disobedience. Disobedience brings problems in individual lives and in relationships as well as in nations. People with perpetual financial problems are usually disobedient to God. Disobedience causes both spiritual and physical famine.

And Joseph died, all his brothers, and all that generation. But the children of Israel were fruitful and increased abundantly, multiplied and grew exceedingly mighty; and the land was filled with them. (Exodus 1:6,7)

God's Word reveals that one of the tactics of Kingdom warfare, taking dominion and subduing the earth, is knowing how to "be fruitful and multiply." The womb that bore many children was blessed. "Happy is the man who has his quiver full of them [children]" (Psalm 127:5). God's Church must consistently birth spiritual children, even as battles are fought and great conflicts erupt.

One philosophy of economic and governmental power is controlling people against their wills by overpowering them. "Dominion" principles teach God-given responsibility through stewardship. The Church must take dominion according to God's ways, not by the forceful influence of worldly philosophies.

Many "kings" who do not know God rule the nations of the earth today. At one time, many kings of European nations honored God. Central and South American rulers once were open and sensitive to the missionary spirit among them. Our forefathers knelt on their knees and prayed unashamedly. Leaders of our armed forces were not too intimidated to get down on their knees, as General George Washington did, and cry out to God for direction.

Today laws even prevent prayer in public schools. An alien spirit that does not know our God dominates society. We live in a land that has almost totally disdained God. Religious educational institutions which were begun by church sponsorship are now producing agnostic or atheistic graduates who are leaders in their fields.

> *And he said to his people, "Look, the people of the children of Israel are more and mightier than we; come, let us deal wisely with them, lest they multiply, and it happen, in the event of war, that they also join our enemies and fight against us, and so go up out of the land." (Exodus 1:9,10)*

Verse nine reveals that the government was concerned about maintaining power over Israel. A competitive spirit dominated their thoughts. That same spirit dominates American culture today.

The Bible says that "the sons of this world are more shrewd in their generation than the sons of light" (Luke 16:8). The world says, "Let's deal wisely in diverting their attention from God. Let's deal wisely with them by confining them with rules and regulations. Let's begin to move in subtle ways to control their lifestyles." That strategy is exactly the way that Satan has maintained control of nations. In Russia, a few revolutionists said, "Let's take control." They began a campaign of appeal to the people. They said, "People, you do not have to be ruled by a selfish monarch." The people responded, "You're right! The czar is bringing great oppression and abuse upon us." The people's army rose up against the czar, and as a result, the people became more abused and oppressed than ever before.

How can we relate that situation to our own individual

choices? Some people complain, "I refuse to be under the discipline of my parents," or "I will not be under the spiritual influence of my church." Rebellion against God's plan always results in the devastation of individuals or governments.

Therefore they set taskmasters over them to afflict them with their burdens. And they built for Pharaoh supply cities, Pithom and Raamses. (Exodus 1:11)

Taskmasters can be taxation systems, zoning laws, or any bureaucracy with no final court of appeals but themselves. Some legislators are now making great efforts to remove tax exemption from the Church. No balance of Christian influence exists in some areas of government to protect the Church's rights.

A few men who control the oil supply of the world also control American lifestyles. When we fill our gas tanks, we actually subject ourselves to the control of that system from another part of the world.

But the more they afflicted them, the more they multiplied and grew. And they were in dread of the children of Israel. So the Egyptians made the children of Israel serve with rigor. And they made their lives bitter with hard bondage—in mortar, in brick, and in all manner of service in the field. All their service in which they made them serve was with rigor. Then the king of Egypt spoke to the Hebrew midwives, of whom the name of one was Shiphrah and the name of the other Puah; and he said, "When you do the duties of a midwife for the Hebrew women, and see them on the birthstools, if it is a son, then you shall kill him; but if it is a daughter, then she shall live." (Exodus 1:12-16)

When Pharaoh noted this multiplication of the Israelites, he decreed a very unique law. **He decided to control the womb.** The two midwives mentioned in this passage serve as a dual witness to Pharaoh for surely more than just two midwives served an entire nation!

Believers should be witnesses in agreement with God, but some Christians are also in agreement with Satan's will. Two people agreeing before God can impact upon world systems, but two negative people can destroy the ministry of a church. Their agreement in negative reports give credibility to one another and sway the opinions of others.

But the midwives feared God, and did not do as the king of Egypt commanded them, but saved the male children alive. (Exodus 1:17)

This passage states a key point. If the midwives were under authority, why did they not obey the king's command? A higher principle of God's will demands obedience to Him above obeying government. When Peter and the disciples were released from prison, they were ordered by authorities not to preach "Jesus Christ." Peter immediately began preaching the gospel again. He responded, "We ought to obey God rather than men" (Acts 5:29). Whenever a conflict arises between government and God's Word, we have no choice other than to obey God, regardless of the personal cost.

So the king of Egypt called for the midwives and said to them, "Why have you done this thing, and saved the male children alive?" And the midwives said to Pharaoh, "Because the Hebrew women are not like the Egyptian women; for they are lively and give birth before the midwives come to them." Therefore God dealt well with the midwives, and the people multiplied and grew very mighty. And so it was, because the midwives feared God, that He provided households for them. (Exodus 1:18-21)

Moses was born into a society in kingdom confrontation (Exodus 2:2). The wilderness experience which followed his leading Israel out of Egypt was a testing period. Every time we move toward God, a testing period immediately begins. After pastoring a church on Euclid Avenue in Atlanta's inner city for five or six years, our ministry met great confrontation. My wife, Norma, my brother, Don, his wife, Clariece, and I ministered to hippies and winos who were coming to our door for help and provisions. Many times I would go to their homes to minister to them. Sometimes as many as thirty or forty people lived in one house. They had confidence in my love for them. They would not hesitate to get me out of bed at night whenever they needed my help.

One night they called on me to pray for a girl who was sick with a fever. I literally crawled on the floor through the crowded room until I found the girl. I reached down and took her in my arms and said, "Honey, Jesus loves you," and ministered to her. One night, as I walked out from one of those times of ministry to "street people" with the stench of poverty and death all around me, I looked up at a starless night. I asked, "God, what in the world is going on? Is this the 'church' You've given to me?" As surely as I have ever heard the voice of God, He answered, "Be faithful."

I do not regard the successes of my ministry in the last twenty-six years as my own accomplishments. The blessings on my church today have come through faithfulness, believing the promises of God and ministry to hurting people. Fulfillment comes as a result of faithfulness in individual lives as well as in ministries. Faithfulness is necessary before God can bring about His will in us. During wilderness periods of testing, we either say like the spies who went into Canaan, "We cannot do it," or we respond like Joshua and Caleb by proclaiming, "We can do it!"

God brought His people to the walls of Jericho. The walls represent religious systems, political systems, and every other system in opposition to God. The only way God could allow His people to be victorious was through spiritual oneness. They were ordered to walk around the walled city seven days—not six, but seven—and to blow their trumpets at a given signal on the seventh day.

The trumpets represent the prophets of God. Walls against God will never fall until God's Church blows one trumpet! God never said that we needed unity of doctrine, but we must come into unity of faith. He didn't say we must all agree in liturgy or forms of worship. He didn't say we must agree in our emphasis or methods in ministry. He said we must agree that "Jesus Christ is Lord" before the walls of confrontation will fall.

A great reaping of the earth will take place when our hearts come into unity before God. We must thank others for truth. Perhaps we don't like someone else's interpretation of certain scripture passages. We may even think certain groups have heresies in their doctrines. Still, we must be open to God and thankful for all truth. We must allow God to "fitly join" us in one declaration of truth to blow a trumpet to the world. Walls fall only when God's people seek the same goals according to God's will, based on faith in Jesus Christ.

Jesus explained clearly how Satan works. Satan comes "to steal, and to kill, and to destroy" (John 10:10). He is a deceiver. People who place burdens on others work against God and become taskmasters who prevent abundant life through Jesus. They may stand tall, look beautiful and sound great, but if they do not follow the principles of God's will in setting people free from bondage, they are opposed to God. They steal virtue from people's lives and destroy trust in hearts. They may have had the presence of God, even as Samson did in his youth, but no longer hear the voice of God or move under an anointing in ministry.

One of Satan's tactics is to appeal to the mind of reason. Satan spoke the mind of reason in the Garden when he said to Eve, ". . . your eyes will be opened, and you will be like God, knowing good and evil" (Genesis 3:5). People say, "Isn't it reasonable that I should have a bigger car and a bigger house?" Satan appeals to our own desires, pressuring us to deny the needs of God's Kingdom as first priority. "So what if God's house is neglected! Who cares if the outreach ministry fails!"

Secondly, Satan attaches burdens to people. He comes subtly saying, "That's just a little drink of wine." Eventually, wine becomes a taskmaster. Alcoholism is a terrible disease, but the devil says, "Go ahead! Drink and enjoy it."

The third tactic of Satan is controlling the supplies that sustain life physically and spiritually. He dictates to farmers, "You cannot grow this. You must grow that. We give you an allotment to grow so much, but you must throw away anything beyond that amount." That philosophy opposes God's plan for planet earth. God never planned for blessed nations to burn wheat and let potatoes rot when people are starving in Mexico, Central America or any other part of the world.

Fourthly, Satan manipulates us to become dependent upon his system of finance. This dependency makes us helpless. He has brought this about through the use of credit cards. People never intend to get into financial difficulty. Even wealthy people have gotten trapped by abusing credit cards. How can God take over the world if we don't allow Him to take over our finances?

The fifth tactic of Satan is to thwart growth patterns. God begins a revival or evangelistic outpouring, and the devil always tries to stop it. Growth is hindered by people who insist that their little church remain small. They shut out new Christians by becoming cliques rather than encouraging all people to experience the love of God's family.

The sixth tactic, one of Satan's most effective tools, is rebellious relationships. Potiphar's wife tried to trap Joseph. Delilah deceived Samson. Herodias was responsible for the order to behead John the Baptist. A damsel stood before Peter and said, "You're one of them." Peter denied it. Within hours, Jesus walked with a reed placed in His hand and blood trickling down His face from the crown of thorns that pierced His brow. As Jesus looked into Peter's eyes, Peter realized what he had done and went out weeping bitterly.

I can imagine Peter, lying on his face before God, crying, "God, if You can forgive me, if You'll just give me one more chance, I won't ever hurt anyone again. I promise always to be true to You. I'll be faithful to my calling. I'll remember who I am."

When the day of Pentecost came, God must have tapped Peter on the shoulder and said, "All right Peter, preach." Peter asked "Who, me?" God reminded Peter of what he had promised in his prayer of repentance. Peter replied that he meant that prayer, and God immediately gave him a message to preach.

Wrong relationships always drive us to experience pain. People we love, even relatives, can demand our allegiances in improper directions. The Bible says to avoid those who come with vile and contentious spirits. Many people are insulated from the dealings of God because people patronize their controlling spirits.

The seventh tactic of Satan is to create a slavery mentality. When the children of Israel were tested in the wilderness, they told Moses they should have remained in slavery. Many people decide that the battle is too difficult and serving God is not worth enduring opposition and accusations.

Satan is a deceiver. Satan is not a lion, but he has a "loud speaker" system. He roars at us every time we follow the leading of the Holy Spirit.

What is our best defense? The best defense is a good offense. We must have a correct knowledge of God's Word. The Bible says that God's people perish for lack of knowledge. We are destroyed unless we are led in the revelation of God. Even Christians will perish in these last days without revelation knowledge. Truth comes by revelation and wisdom from God's Word. Revelation is conveyed by the Holy Spirit, but it is also demonstrated in our lives by the power of God.

A good defense requires a pure heart before God. Our motives for serving the Lord should be examined daily. We are either submitted to God or Satan. We must take the responsibility for searching our hearts. God knows when our motives are aggressive and competitive. We know our own hearts only by opening ourselves to God's admonition. "For the word of God is living and powerful, and sharper than any two-edged sword, piercing even to the division of soul and spirit, and of joints and marrow, and is a discerner of the thoughts and intents of the heart" (Hebrews 4:12).

When the Spirit of God reveals that our motives are wrong, we must immediately correct them through prayer, or our households and callings will be in spiritual jeopardy. Problems are small when compared to God's judgment. God isn't influenced by the faces of men. A person can appear to be spiritually attuned when inside he is as rotten as hell. Discerning people cannot be fooled by surface appearances.

A correct mentality is necessary to become obedient to God. Genuine obedience of faith, like that demonstrated by Shadrach, Meshach and Abednego, will not bow to the gods of this world. A mentality such as Stephen had will cause one to pray for his enemies while enduring their abuse even to death.

"The fool has said in his heart, 'There is no God' " (Psalm 53:1). A modern interpretation of that verse is, "The fool has said in his heart, 'I don't want spiritual authority. I'm tired of being told what to do. I don't want to be controlled anymore. I don't want God or His direction.' " Eventually God will honor that request and turn people over to reprobate minds. They will think they're acting out of sincerity, but they will be going straight to hell.

Using positive spiritual tools is essential. What are positive tools? Praying for enemies! Doing good in return for evil! Rejoicing in tribulation! Positive tools include making peace, reconciling the wounded and pouring the oil and wine of healing.

We will confront spiritual walls like the walled city of Jericho when we attempt reconciliation. But God's Church cannot attack the systems of this world if we are divided among ourselves. Many religious organizations are mere skeletons without the power of God.

The mighty prophet, Ezekiel, saw scattered bones representing God's Church today. Presbyterians, Methodists, Charismatics, Catholics and others raise walls of division that scatter the influence and effectiveness of the body of Christ. God said to prophesy and His Word of prophecy will bring scattered bones together. As the Spirit of God and the spirit of prophecy move over those bones, the bones will snap together miraculously. Each bone remained in its own place of identity, but they joined together. They began to join ranks as Ezekiel saw a mighty army stand up and march.

God is beginning to move in these last days. This is harvest time. The time has come for the sickle to be thrust into the earth. The hour for reaping of the earth is at hand. God is saying, "Blow your trumpets, prophets! Examine the truth given by the ancient church fathers. Consider the truth of the Reformation period, the Whitfield and Wesleyan revivals, the traditional Pentecostal movement, the fundamentalist Baptist groups, the Calvinistic Presbysterians. Observe liturgy and appreciate the solemn, sacred sacraments that the Catholic Church has preserved. See what each group is really saying! Heed the message of deliverance and healing!" God is proclaiming through His prophets that His Kingdom is about to be manifested like never before. We must receive all truth. Instead of a judgmental attitude toward a vessel bringing truth, we must say, "God, let the trumpets of truth sound as one voice in the earth!"

Joshua's army marched around the wall under command. They started walking toward the opposition. As they walked, the ground under their feet began to shake.

The Bible says that everything that can be shaken will be shaken. But what will remain? What will not be shaken? The only thing unshaken at Jericho was the people walking for God in unity. Unity of purpose in God's people will not be shaken.

We must press toward systems of economics, athletics, politics, the arts and education with the intention of possessing their territory. Sounds of soldiers marching, trumpets sounding and drums beating from another realm call us together as we begin marching as God's mighty army, God's family. Babylon is falling! In the midst of confrontations, the Kingdom of God will be established in its fullness.

6

CHAPTER SIX

God has begun to clarify the time of harvest. Certain events signifying this long-awaited time have been taught for years. Expectations emphasized by my classical Pentecostal background of dispensationalism consist of earthquakes, famines and diseases. These cataclysmic events are pertinent to the end-times, but I believe that God is giving us fresh anointing to understand the panoramic scope of the time of harvest.

The signs of the time of harvest do not focus on negative events like wars, pestilence and earthquakes, which Christians previously anticipated as signs. Jesus said, "All these are but the beginning of sorrows" (Matthew 24:8). Coinciding with the period of cataclysmic events in the natural realm, we also enter into the age of harvest.

Jesus said, "Do not worry about the times nor the seasons." He made this statement in order to emphasize that the Kingdom will come in power (Acts 1:8). Under the anointing of God, the Apostle Paul said, "But you, brethren, are not in darkness, so that this Day should overtake you as a thief" (I Thessalonians 5:4).

The following scripture gives insights that have frequently been overlooked.

> *Another parable He put forth to them, saying: "The kingdom of heaven is like a man who sowed good seed in his field; but while men slept, his enemy came and sowed tares among the wheat and went his way. But when the grain had sprouted and produced a crop, then the tares also appeared. So the servants of the owner came and said to him, 'Sir, did you not sow good seed in your field? How then does it have tares?' He said to them, 'An enemy has done this.' The servants said to him, 'Do you want us then to go and gather them up?' But he said, 'No, lest while you gather up the tares you also uproot the wheat with them. Let both grow together **until** the harvest, and at the time of harvest I will say to the reapers, "First gather together the tares and bind them in bundles to burn them, but gather the wheat into my barn." ' " (Matthew 13:24-30)*

The word "until" becomes more and more important as we read Scripture with prophetic understanding. Jesus said to let the wheat and tares grow together "until" the harvest. I recently wrote a book entitled *Held in the Heavens Until . . .* referring to the meaning of Acts 3:21 which says concerning Jesus, ". . . whom heaven must receive **until** the times of restoration of all things, which God has spoken by the mouth of all His holy prophets since the world began." The word "until" in scripture indicates that God waits for obedient people to fulfill His plan.

But when He [Jesus] saw the multitudes, He was moved with compassion for them, because they were weary and scattered, like sheep having no shepherd. Then He said to His disciples, "The harvest truly is plentiful, but the laborers are few. Therefore pray the Lord of the harvest to send out laborers into His harvest." (Matthew 9:36-38)

We are the ongoing incarnation of Christ who sow and reap spiritual seed. The Apostle Paul quoted Isaiah. ". . . How beautiful are the feet of those who preach the gospel of peace, who bring glad tidings of good things!" (Romans 10:15).

Two kingdoms are in continuous conflict. The kingdom of darkness opposes the kingdom of light; the sons of the enemy battle the sons of the Kingdom. I proclaim to you that we have come to the time of harvest, the end of the age. The gospel of the Kingdom will separate those who practice lawlessness from those whose witness will shine like the sun.

Therefore as the tares are gathered and burned in the fire, so it will be at the end of this age. The Son of Man will send out His angels, and they will gather out of His kingdom all things that offend, and those who practice lawlessness, and will cast them into the furnace of fire. There will be wailing and gnashing of teeth. Then the righteous will shine forth as the sun in the kingdom of their Father. He who has ears to hear, let him hear! (Matthew 13:40-43)

The book of Revelation makes it clear that John

wrote his letters to the angels of the Church. Who are the angels that God will use? They are ministers called by God to boldly proclaim the Word of God. They will sound the trumpet. One should never separate prophecy of the New Testament from prophetic Old Testament scriptures. The trumpet sounded in the Old Testament as a warning. Today the trumpet sounds from the angels of the Church, God's ministers who cry out, "It is harvest time!" Witnesses to God's power will shine as never before. God will gather righteous people together to raise up a witness of Jesus Christ and judge the kingdoms of this world.

The first sign of the time of harvest is an answer to Jesus' prayer in John 17. ". . . that they all may be one just as We are one," speaking of His people, the Church. Jesus prayed, "Father, make them one so the world may know."

Before the world can see the "witness" of the Kingdom, God must bring unity and oneness to the body of Christ. Unity will never occur through organizational structure but only through the movements of the Holy Spirit. A move toward unity among ministries is occurring around the world where men and women of God interact on a spiritual level of exchange. They recognize that this is God's time of harvest.

On January 21, 1986, in Dallas, Texas, twenty-seven trustees and founders of the Charismatic Bible Ministries gathered to experience extraordinary oneness of spirit. This fraternal joining of men and women of God from the Charismatic movement came together to express love. Together, we intend to take the gospel of deliverance of our Savior Jesus Christ to this generation.

The members sharing together with founders Oral and Evelyn Roberts were: Jack Hayford, Richard Roberts, James Buskirk, Lester Sumrall, Tommy Barnett, Karl Strader, Happy Caldwell, Stephen Strang, Jerry Savelle, Kenneth Copeland, Kenneth Hagin, John Meares, Buddy Harrison, John Osteen, Jamie Buckingham, Freda Lindsay, Marilyn Hickey, Vinson Synan, Tommy Reid, John Gimenez, Mike Murdock, Billy Joe Daugherty, Robert Tilton, Hilton Sutton and me. Pastor Paul Yonggi Cho is the international representative for this network of ministries.

Oral Roberts emphasized that the body of Christ will move by signs and wonders in the last days. I believe the spirit of Elijah will come upon the Church with great, undeniable signs and wonders. Since the first requirement to bring about the time of the harvest is oneness in the body of Christ, enemies of the Lord will claim that unity exists only among a small, scattered group. I respond by saying that God is bringing together not only old-line Pentecostals and Charismatics, but many other Christians in His body as well.

Dr. Frank Harrington, pastor of Peachtree Presbyterian Church, Dr. Bill Self, pastor of Wieuca Road Baptist Church, and I jointly hosted Dr. Robert Schuller's Leadership Seminar in Atlanta in April 1986. We have joined together in this thrust to promote Christian unity in our city. A communion service, in which members of our three congregations shared at the end of the seminar, was a special, memorable event

creating unshakable bonds of love. The need for oneness in the body of Christ is obvious. Old walls of
separation among God's people are truly beginning to
crumble.

Year-round conferences convening directly out of
this ministry include Latin and Central American and
Caribbean pastors and Church leaders. The dominant
feeling is that this is God's time for the body of Christ to
be strong in oneness. That urgency is a major sign to
the world that we are in "harvest time."

The disciples came to Jesus and said, "Lord, these
thousands of people are hungry. What are we going to
do?" Jesus had been teaching the people in a desert
place, just as this world is a spiritual desert. Jesus used
a young lad's lunch consisting of two fish and five
loaves of bread to feed the people. The two fish represent agreement of two "as touching anything . . ." The
five loaves of bread represent the bread of life, the
five-fold ministry. These are the tools that God will also
use in His strategy to feed the multitudes spiritually.
God always sends a lad, someone willing to give God
whatever provisions or talents he has. My, what a prophetic story this is!

**The second sign of the "time of harvest" is
world systems and world governments being
shaken today as never before.** The book of Hebrews
describes the day in which we live.

*See that you do not refuse Him who speaks. For if they did
not escape who refused Him who spoke on earth, much
more shall we not escape if we turn away from Him who
speaks from heaven, whose voice then shook the earth;
but now He has promised, saying, "Yet once more I shake*

not only the earth, but also heaven." Now this, "Yet once more," indicates the removal of those things that are being shaken, as of things that are made, that the things which cannot be shaken may remain. Therefore, since we are receiving a kingdom which cannot be shaken, let us have grace, by which we may serve God acceptably with reverence and godly fear. (Hebrews 12:25-28)

Tremendous political, economic and social upheavals occur daily around the world. Only things that cannot be shaken—the systems ruled by the Holy Spirit—will remain. Worldly systems will fall apart.

The Kingdom of God begins in our personal lives. Christ cannot rule our cities until He rules the lives of Christians who live in the cities. Christ must rule in Christians' lifestyles before Babylon will fall.

Then a mighty angel took up a stone like a great millstone and threw it into the sea, saying, "Thus with violence the great city Babylon shall be thrown down, and shall not be found anymore. The sound of harpists, musicians, flutists, and trumpeters shall not be heard in you anymore. And no craftsman of any craft shall be found in you anymore. And the sound of a millstone shall not be heard in you anymore. And the light of a lamp shall not shine in you anymore. And the voice of bridegroom and bride shall not be heard in you anymore. For your merchants were the great men of the earth, for by your sorcery all the nations were deceived. And in her was found the blood of prophets and saints, and of all who were slain on the earth." (Revelation 18:21-24)

A great death rattle sounds today. I am amused by Satan's big roar when he is about to be defeated. Satan is roaring loudly because he realizes that we are preparing for harvest time. More and more, we are going to hear his death rattles.

Satan's most successful tactic is fear. Terrorism and lawlessness prevail in the Philippines, the Mideast and Central America because of fear. Many places of the world lack any type of control, creating widespread tyranny, fear and intimidation.

We must recognize the death rattles of Satan. Terrorists attacking airports around the world, unknown murderers putting glass in baby food or tampering with aspirin capsules sold commercially are tools Satan uses to perpetrate widespread fear. Fear tactics are aimed at churches even by the Internal Revenue Service. But we have news for Satan and his army. Their day is short! The power of God is about to bring them to final judgment!

Ask financial experts about the security of our banking system. If we lay up treasures only in material things, we are already in trouble. We need to start investing financially in the lives of our boys and girls. We need to invest in Christian education and in things that will insure rewards in heavenly places.

Three spirits have been released upon planet earth. The first is the **spirit of atheism** which is a ruler spirit to humanistic philosophy which I have discussed. Atheism creates confusion in religion and causes masses of people to conclude that no one has the answers to life's questions.

The **spirit of lawlessness** is the second spirit. The Bible says that in the last days ". . . lawlessness will abound, the love of many will grow cold" (Matthew 24:12).

Lawlessness is a ruler spirit to rebellion. I have great confidence in God's people, but not in the ability of people to govern themselves. The Word of God does not condone being a king unto oneself! The real theme of such a generation is "I did it my way—under no one's control, submitting to no one."

The **spirit of mammon** is the third spirit that controls our world today. Atheism, lawlessness and mammon are the spirits of the day. Latin American countries and other places in great turmoil are plagued with spirits that have been released from Satan. Like the frogs described in Revelation, we are living right in the middle of the plagues John said would take place. John said that satanic forces would go out over the whole earth (Revelation 16:13,14). Humanism and vain philosophies dominate social thinking.

Now as He sat on the Mount of Olives, the disciples came to Him privately, saying, "Tell us, when will these things be? And what will be the sign of Your coming, and of the end of the age?" And Jesus answered and said to them: "Take heed that no one deceives you. For many will come in My name, saying, 'I am the Christ,' and will deceive many." (Matthew 24:3-5)

Another significant sign of the time of reaping refers to organizations insisting that they are "Christ." An example is certain denominations claiming that they alone are right on doctrine and everyone else is wrong. The fellowship of Charismatic Bible Ministries is dedicated to breaking down those prejudices and leaping over the walls that separate God's children.

And you will hear of wars and rumors of wars. See that you are not troubled; for all these things must come to pass, but the end is not yet. For nation will rise against nation, and kingdom against kingdom. And there will be famines, pestilences, and earthquakes in various places. All these are the beginning of sorrows. Then they will deliver you up to tribulation and kill you, and you will be hated by all nations for My name's sake. And then many will be offended, will betray one another, and will hate one another. Then many false prophets will rise up and deceive many. (Matthew 24:6-11)

Kingdom against kingdom is the third sign. The Church is entering into its greatest tests of tribulation. God's people will be hated by all nations because they are challenging nations, governments and systems. They will be hated because they have found answers that resolve chaotic dilemmas. Joseph personifies this age. Joseph finally triumphed over those who despised him because he had answers.

People crying out against the Church and labeling God's messengers "false prophets" do not know the difference between deceit and truth. Accusations against the Church are voiced by people who confuse the teachings of the occult and Eastern religions with biblical answers. Accusers attribute the beginning of "mind power" to the occult. That accusation is false. God fashioned "mind power" when he created man, placed him in the Garden and told him to subdue the earth. Some people try to build doctrines on the counterfeit rather than truth. Find out what God said originally in His Word, then proclaim, "Thus saith the Lord!"

Kingdom confrontation is a sign of the final time of harvest. The greatest confrontations ever known will

110

be political. Separation will occur between those called of God to govern by the Spirit of God and those pursuing positions because of their own aggressive spirits and desire for fame and power.

Clashes between humanism and Christianity will accelerate. Some public servants will take bold stands for Christian ethics. Other politicians will espouse humanism. This diversity will be evident in upcoming national elections.

We cannot miss God's will! For every confrontation, God has a man and God has a plan. We must recognize God's plan and His man for a particular area of service and then pray to determine our course of action in supporting that leader.

Confrontations in the area of the arts will be strong. Great confrontation will occur between artistic designs that are of God, expressing His creation, and those that are not. The music industry will continue to experience great warfare. Evil musicians will infiltrate the Church. Men and women on whom God has placed His anointing in music must be very keen in discerning where God wants them to serve and use their talents.

Kingdom confrontations will accelerate in the field of education. As the government gets more involved in pressuring private educational institutions, public education will struggle to survive. The only hope for future generations is God's Church involved in education. Solomon's and Sheba's kingdoms illustrate the difference between societies. A queen came to see the kingdom that Solomon had built according to God's instructions and wisdom. She was awed by the things she observed. The queen said, "The half has never been told!"

Jesus said, ". . . The harvest truly is plentiful, but the laborers are few. Therefore pray the Lord of the harvest to send out laborers into His harvest" (Matthew 9:37,38). God will enlist people who are willing to say, "Count me in! I am a businessman and I will turn my training over to God. I am a social worker and I will use my skills for God. I am a person in the arts. I give my talents totally to the Lord." Tremendous anointing will come to those who say, "Let me be a part of what God is doing!"

God's strategy to reclaim the earth is to build cities. Eden, a city, was the location of the "Garden." "The Lord God planted a garden eastward in Eden . . ." (Genesis 2:8). Eden was a city of law, order and social activities. A city is people, not buildings. If every building in Atlanta disappeared, it would still be a city because people live there.

Eden was God's idea, a city where He placed the Garden. Cain lived in the land of Nod on the east of Eden (Genesis 4:16,17). God is networking spiritual headship in cities around the world today. When God establishes spiritual headship in cities, a tremendous reaping will result. Authorities will seek out the spiritual heads even as the king searched for the prophet Elijah because he had the power to command rain. Leaders will try to find the people who are in touch with "the rain giver."

> *Cush begot Nimrod; he began to be a mighty one on the earth. He was a mighty hunter before the Lord; therefore it is said, "Like Nimrod the mighty hunter before the Lord."*

And the beginning of his kingdom was Babel, Erech, Accad, and Calneh, in the land of Shinar. From that land he went to Assyria and built Nineveh, Rehoboth Ir, Calah . . . (Genesis 10:8-11)

This story explains the beginning of cities. Many city builders were against God, while others never even considered God. Nimrod built the city of Nineveh from the fruits of Babel. People gathered in a "city spirit" in the plain of Shinar to build Nineveh. Later, God sent His prophet Jonah to Nineveh. The same strategy that brought Nineveh to repentance will work today. An anointed prophet of God, a city that prays and fasts and city leadership bowing before God in repentance will bring revival anywhere in the world.

I am concerned about politics and legislative action, but cities of the world do not belong to governmental leaders. Cities belong to God and people. I am weary with people who are insensitive to God's voice. God wants leaders who will listen and implement whatever He wants accomplished in cities.

Abraham looked for a city "whose builder and maker was God" (Hebrews 11:10). God wants us to understand His ways of order and personal interaction. God is not against cities. He said, "O Jerusalem, I love you." He is not against Atlanta or New York. He is against worldly systems that control the direction of activities within cities.

For here we have no continuing city, but we seek the one to come. (Hebrews 13:14)

Scripture tells of the heavenly city, the New Jerusalem,

a city that will come down from above. The scriptures are not describing some planet coming down from the sky like a big cube. John used symbolic language. The New Jerusalem refers to the "city" who are the people of God. Jerusalem refers to "the people who were not a people." They are birthed from the spirit realm. The Bible speaks of a "Jerusalem below" and the "Jerusalem above." God is building a city where Christ rules and reigns. The followers of Christ are a city set upon a hill, a witness city. Jesus said,

> *You are the light of the world. A city that is set on a hill cannot be hidden. Nor do they light a lamp and put it under a basket, but on a lampstand, and it gives light to all who are in the house. Let your light so shine before men, that they may see your good works and glorify your Father in heaven. (Matthew 5:14-16)*

I believe that Chapel Hill is part of that eternal city. I believe Tommy Reid speaks to part of that city in Buffalo, New York. I believe Happy Caldwell leads some of that city in Little Rock, Arkansas. Tommy Barnett is a pastor to part of it in Phoenix, Arizona, and many other parts of that eternal city shine around the world. God said, "Build witness cities. Witness against any city which refuses My truth." Christ will not come until His Church acts and moves under His power to become a properly governed city. Prejudice, bigotry and competition within God's Church prevent the return of Christ. People controlled by their egos ask, "What part am I going to get? Who is going to sit on the right and on the left?" Remember, we must be city dwellers, fitly joined together with unique talents and abilities. Everyone among us is important. Working with children, parking cars, maintaining church property, directing traffic—all are vital services to the King.

Jesus said that witness cities shine to the world. The world will ask, "How do you take care of elderly people? How do you take care of girls who are pregnant out of wedlock? How do you minister to people who are suicidal?" God's churches must become witness cities, set upon hills to challenge the systems of this world.

The New Jerusalem coming down from God out of heaven will be the alliance or culmination of all witness cities. God's people will become the glorious New Jerusalem when Christ Himself comes to rule and reign on earth. Christ will come again, just as He went away. Where is He going to sit? In Jerusalem? The Bible says that every eye shall behold Him. It doesn't matter where He returns geographically, just that He comes. People worry about things that are meaningless in relation to God's will for them today.

Jesus Christ will come only when the glorious city of Jerusalem becomes a reality in our hearts. That city will be governed by a loving God who has totally conquered worldly spirits. Those who rule in the city of God will understand overcoming by love, not by firearms or terrorism. Total victory comes by the power of love.

How did Christ overcome world systems? He loved them. They persecuted Him, and yet He continued to love them. He even loved those who rejected Him and mocked His kingship with a crown of thorns. Spiritual cities must be governed with the power of love.

Vicarious love carries its own cross, a strategy from the heart of God. Why did Jesus carry His own cross? Vicarious love loses sight of ambitions and desires. Vicarious love suffers in the interest of others by carrying a cross for their sakes. Jesus said, "If anyone desires to come after Me, let him deny himself, and take up his cross, and follow me" (Matthew 16:24). When Jesus was crucified on the cross and the last drop of blood drained from His body, the earth quaked. Even the elements showed disapproval at His suffering. The Roman centurion spoke the dynamic words, "Truly this was the Son of God!" (Matthew 27:54). We may be persecuted or imprisoned, but eventually our captors will say, "They showed us God's way."

Only the power of the cross will overcome the enemies' rule. Vicarious love does not necessarily mean walking up and down the sidewalk carrying a protest sign. Silence can speak loudly against certain issues. If God wants action, we must willingly observe His will. God is calling for a new understanding of the "power in love" principle that has never been fully understood or demonstrated by the Church.

How is that city to be governed? We demonstrate strength through submission.

For to this you were called, because Christ also suffered for us, leaving us an example, that you should follow His steps: "Who committed no sin, nor was guile found in His mouth"; who, when He was reviled, did not revile in return; when He suffered, He did not threaten, but committed Himself to Him who judges righteously; who Himself bore our sins in His own body on the tree, that we, having died to sins, might live for righteousness—by whose stripes you were healed. (I Peter 2:21-24)

Wives must be in subjection to their husbands, their own spiritual headship. People who are employed must understand the reasons they are working in relation to Kingdom goals. Through excellent work habits and a servant spirit, others will be brought to Christ. When we do God's will and yet suffer for some reason, we must maintain patience. Christ also suffered. A spirit of willing submission brings strength. Jesus said, "My strength is made perfect in weakness" (II Corinthians 12:9).

Harvest will occur only when we demonstrate the overcoming power of God.

> *... that you may become blameless and harmless, children of God without fault in the midst of a crooked and perverse generation, among whom you shine as lights in the world, holding fast the word of life, so that I may rejoice in the day of Christ that I have not run in vain or labored in vain. (Philippians 2:15,16)*

Jesus Christ was equal with God (Philippians 2:6), yet Jesus chose a lowly position and became a servant. If we can understand the principle of servanthood, we will also experience Kingdom power and authority.

Harvest will never occur until Christians learn the true meaning of prayer. The world needs praying churches. In some churches, the entire congregation assembles early in the morning to pray. Without being judgmental by generalizing, some spiritual exercises can become works of the flesh. Jesus said that for some prayers, we should go into a "closet" place, closing ourselves away from public observation. Praying in secret is rewarded openly. "If two of you agree on earth concerning anything that they ask, it will be done for them by My Father in heaven" (Matthew 18:19). God's Word says that we must learn the strength of agreement. Quality prayer gives reality to "binding the strongman." He said to pray, "Thy Kingdom come, Thy will be done." How do we pray? Novices pray primarily for their own needs, but spiritual warriors bind the strongman.

Certain spirits dominate cities, although the same ones do not control every city. God gives understanding to identify these spirits. One of the strong spirits over our city, Atlanta, Georgia, is pride in accomplishments. A slogan identifying Atlanta states that we are "A City Too Busy To Hate."

Called intercessors identify and bind the strongman before He plunders the house. They intercede at the altars of Almighty God amid adversity until they touch the desires of God's heart.

Agreement never comes through tongues of praise; agreement comes through tongues of intercession. The Spirit of praise and worship is enjoyed by the masses. The heart of the intercessor stands singular before God.

> *Therefore, since we are receiving a kingdom which cannot be shaken, let us have grace, by which we may serve God acceptably with reverence and godly fear. (Hebrews 12:28)*

A church unwilling to minister grace cannot be used in end-time ministry. One of the greatest problems with a "holiness mentality" is a condescending attitude and a judgmental spirit. God's Church must be purged from guilt and fear. The Church today understands restoration of lost sheep but seldom extends restoration to shepherds also. Sheep should do the restoring. Sheep bear wool, and wool provides both warmth and substance or revenue. God is saying, "By grace, I will show strength in My Church. You will know how to lift people from defeat and put them back on the right path."

Feelings of fear are inappropriate during harvest time. If we know the God who controls the fire, we need not worry about destructive fires. If we know the God who created the lion, we don't have to fear the lion's den. If we know the God who controls the jail, we don't need to worry about the jailer. This mentality projects the assurance that our God is able to shelter us in any circumstance of life.

People who move with God don't worry about world systems, because He that is within us is greater than he that is in the world. We need to harvest every kingdom with rapidity and proclaim boldly, "The Kingdom of God is at hand!"

This is the hour, the day of confrontation and proclamation. If we fail to perform God's will, He will move on to someone else. Jesus wept over the city of Jerusalem saying, "You did not know the time of your visitation" (Luke 19:44). We get involved in power struggles, debate who is going to sit where, and who is going to be called by what title. Meanwhile, we could miss our visitation from God. I believe that people who hear what God is saying can accomplish whatever is necessary to manifest the witness in this generation.

Romans controlled Palestine. The Romans built fortresses and places for their armies to dwell on the tops of the hills. History records that fires surrounded the city at night, signifying to all the people that the Roman Empire was in control. Jesus saw those fires and said, "I will build My people as a city on a hilltop to shine their lights before men, to show their good works."

God will have a lighthouse, a standard, by which He will judge world systems. That mission must determine the decisions in any ministry that God will use to reap the earth. God has called us to be a city of refuge. He has called us to be a city of truth and light, a witness city, proclaiming the Kingdom of God.

Men must learn to work together. God does not want us doing "our own thing"; He is concerned about our doing "His thing." His city does not consist of land and buildings, but people witnessing love, justice, righteousness and joy in their lives. That is the city God is building. God wants open hearts and humble spirits. He will not tolerate complaining, ego-hungry spirits as Kingdom builders. He wants men and women seeking first the Kingdom of God, doing His work with all of their hearts.

7
CHAPTER SEVEN

The work of God is not finished, but it is being completed through the Church. The work of redemption was completed in Jesus Christ. Then Christ left us with a commission, a challenge, an assignment to complete. The finished work of Calvary is now being lived out in the world. God's redemptive process includes all creatures dwelling upon the planet, as well as planet earth itself. Each one of us fits into God's plan. We are "fitly joined together" to fulfill His purposes on earth. God's original intentions in creation cannot be separated from events taking place in the world today.

After Jesus encountered the Samaritan woman, He spoke of the "whitened harvest."

In the meantime His disciples urged Him, saying, "Rabbi, eat." But He said to them, "I have food to eat of which you do not know." Therefore the disciples said to one another, "Has anyone brought Him anything to eat?" Jesus said to them, "My food is to do the will of Him who sent Me, and to finish His work. Do you not say, 'There are still four months and then comes the harvest'? Behold, I say to you, lift up your eyes and look at the fields, for they are already white for harvest! And he who reaps receives wages, and gathers fruit for eternal life, that both he who sows and he who reaps may rejoice together. For in this the saying is true: 'One sows and another reaps.' I sent you to reap that for which you have not labored; others have labored, and you have entered into their labors." (John 4:31-38)

This scripture defines the strategy to finish God's work. Jesus said that His food—His existence and purpose—was to do the will of His Father who sent Him.

When Jesus said, "I have food that you know not of," He was declaring that He lived in a different dimension than His disciples. We, too, must move beyond the natural planes of our own existence—beyond flat tires, dripping faucets, leaky roofs and family quarrels. Each Christian must answer these questions for himself: "What is my food [sustenance]? What is my reason for living? What is God's calling to me as one created in His very likeness?"

Our first priority, regardless of who we are—daddy, mother, boy, girl—is to hear and do the will of our Father. We must understand that we don't live just to build a big house, make money or develop relationships. All these things pass away. As Jesus said, "This

[My Father's will] is the fruit of **eternal** life," fruit that does not die but yields everlasting rewards. We must live to find out why God put us here and how we fit into His plan.

Our second priority is to finish our Father's work. From the time God said, "I will create man in My likeness and in My image," He gave man dominion, power of research, power of productivity and creative authority. From the time God incorporated man into His work until now, mankind has been in a process of discovering God's intentions. I firmly believe that God created man in His effort to correct something that had gone wrong in His plan for the universe. Scriptures tell us that the world was "without form and void." Something had gone wrong that required man's efforts— empowered by the Holy Spirit—to correct.

Jesus gave a fairly simple strategy for doing the Father's work when He said, ". . . look at the fields, for they are **already** white for harvest!" Who has not noticed that the world is looking for answers? Who has not observed political confusion and countries in absolute devastation? The world is seeking solutions which only the people of God can supply as we begin to sow seeds of the Kingdom of God.

Jesus was slain from the foundation of the world because God knew that mankind required redemption. As God's "new" creation through Jesus Christ, we have shared in His plan to recover this planet since the very beginning. We are inseparably tied to what God is going to do in the world. Somehow, we got sidetracked into thinking that God's only concern was bringing us to spiritual redemption. We thought eternal salvation freed us of any further responsibility. We must now readdress the fact that we serve as an integral part of fulfilling the desires of God's heart, even moving as His witnesses in implementing our Father's will.

When requests were made of Jesus, He often answered by saying that He and God worked together to accomplish His Father's will (John 5:17). That response is the same for Christians today. Jesus said, "It is expedient that I go away so the Holy Spirit will come and enable you to become a part of My Father's plan. I have finished the work of redemption. Now you must take the authority of the Holy Spirit and move with the Father to finish His work." We are not only God's workmanship, but we are also a vital part of fulfilling the purposes of God's master plan.

What is the mind of God for this day?

They answered and said to Him, "Abraham is our father." Jesus said to them, "If you were Abraham's children, you would do the works of Abraham. But now you seek to kill Me, a Man who has told you the truth which I heard from God. Abraham did not do this. You do the deeds of your father." Then they said to Him, "We were not born of fornication; we have one Father—God." Jesus said to them, "If God were your Father, you would love Me, for I proceeded forth and came from God; nor have I come of Myself, but He sent Me. Why do you not understand My speech? Because you are not able to listen to My word. You are of your father the devil, and the desires of your father you want to do. He was a murderer from the beginning, and does not stand in the truth, because there is no truth in him. When he speaks a lie, he speaks from his own resources, for he is a liar and the father of it." (John 8:39-44)

The word "fornication," as Jesus used it here, is a spiritual term which has nothing to do with a carnal relationship. Jesus used "fornication" to describe a spiritual intimacy with the world. Mixtures do exist in the Church today. We must apply the purging power of the Word of God by the Holy Spirit to purify our witness.

We live as products serving one of two spirits at work in the world today. If we are a product of Satan, who is a liar, we are contributing members of a reprobate society. If we are a product of our Father God, we become implementers of His will. His Word sustains us as our "food" night and day. We either belong to Satan or to God. For that reason, the new birth is absolutely necessary to move us from the kingdom of darkness into the Kingdom of light.

> *For by grace you have been saved through faith, and that not of yourselves; it is the gift of God, not of works, lest anyone should boast. (Ephesians 2:8,9)*

In this passage, Paul is not referring to "the works" of the Father, that is, implementing God's will. He is speaking of salvation, a gift of grace from God. Many people become confused because they believe that salvation is a gift that carries no price or responsibility with it. Salvation **is** a free gift. But after we enter into covenant with God, works become absolutely necessary to enter His Kingdom. We cannot be in covenant with God without demonstrating works of faith.

> *For we are His workmanship, created in Christ Jesus for good works, which God prepared beforehand that we should walk in them. (Ephesians 2:10)*

God created us expressly for good works. We must never allow the devil to tell us that we can see God and live with Him eternally without works of faith. That promise simply is not recorded in God's Word. James even said, "Show me your faith without your works, and I will show you my faith by my works" (James 2:18).

> *. . . having made known to us the mystery of His will, according to His good pleasure which He purposed in Himself. (Ephesians 1:9)*

When we find the mystery of God's will, we will know the strategy that will enable us to finish God's work. Jesus said, "I came to finish the work of the Father." As the body of Christ in the world today, we enter into finishing that work.

> *. . . that in the dispensation of the fullness of the times He might gather together in one all things in Christ, both which are in heaven and which are on earth—in Him, in whom also we have obtained an inheritance, being pre-destined according to the purpose of Him who works all things according to the counsel of His will. . . (Ephesians 1:10,11)*

In order to participate in God's moving upon this planet, we must understand that the mystery of His will has now been revealed. Jesus Christ is gathering together all things in heaven and in earth and combining them into a single plan that cures the ills of the universe. Everything that has gone wrong is now being corrected in Jesus Christ—governments, education, the arts—**everything** is gathered back under

God in Jesus Christ, as His people witness to His standards in those areas.

Salvation is beautifully expressed in God's Word: "For God so loved the world . . ." (John 3:16). God loved **all** things. In His love for the world, Jesus told us to pray, "Thy Kingdom come **on earth** as it is **in heaven** . . ." We are fitly joined together even now with the heavenly congregation because we are ". . . compassed around about with a great cloud of witnesses." All of heaven and earth yearn for the implementation of God's will. The work of God will be finished when the earth is restored to the dominion of Jesus Christ. That is the mystery of His will. The call to God's Church everywhere is to bring all things under God's authority by demonstrating His standards in every area as a witness. When that mission is completed, we can present that accomplishment to God as His work completed.

God has given us the Holy Spirit to help us. He has given us an example of His standard, the firstfruit, in Jesus Christ. I am sure that God will effect some aspects of our witness through divine intervention. I believe that His intervention on behalf of Shadrach, Meshach and Abednego is a foreshadowing of His intervention for His Church in days to come.

The time has come when God wants His saints in unity and love with such a deep understanding of His authority that in the midst of a worship service we can proclaim, "God is now accomplishing a miraculous work in this congregation. Everyone here is going to be healed. There will be no infirmities among us." Impossible? I don't think so. When the virtue of Jesus Christ begins to flow, all things are possible.

Brother Oral Roberts said that he saw a twelve-minute manifestation of a mighty move of the power of God take place in Jacksonville, Florida, several years ago. He said the Spirit of God came upon him and said, "I have commanded a total healing for this congregation." Over a twelve-minute period, every wheelchair emptied. Those using crutches laid them down. The deaf began to hear; the blind began to see. After twelve minutes, the manifestation ended.

Why should the power of God be precisely timed? "Twelve" signifies the Trinity involved with the four corners of the earth—God involved with His creation. I believe those minutes symbolized God's desire to interact with His Church today. This is God's hour to divinely intervene in our behalf. But we must do our part or God cannot help us.

God's divine order—the Kingdom of God—has existed since the beginning. The Kingdom is not a new concept; it is as everlasting as God Himself. Lucifer fell from his appointed place in creation as he attempted to exalt himself above God. Because Lucifer's fall resulted in formlessness and void on the earth, God said, "I will fill that emptiness with My creation. I will make man in My image, and he will fill the void." From that very hour, God's plan was that His people might fill that vacancy. Since Lucifer was the god of worship and praise, we now must fill that void. We must become the habitation of God's praise and worship. Where Satan created darkness and confusion, Jesus said, "I am the Light of the world." Now He says to us, "**You are the Light of the world.**" An antidote for every darkness that Lucifer caused in society is found in God's Church, shining as a light to a darkened world.

The Church replaces Lucifer in worship. Therefore, our worship impacts the heavenly realm. Whatever we loose on earth, by God's power and goodness and love, He will loose in heaven. Authority to bind and loose is the key to the Kingdom. Heaven and earth interact so that we can bring heaven's laws to bear upon the earth. That is the reason Jesus said, "Pray, Thy Kingdom come, Thy will be done on earth as it is in heaven."

Interaction between heaven and earth is essential to reaping the harvest. Spiritual interaction between heaven and earth is not mysticism. A fine line separates genuine interaction by the Spirit which glorifies God from a counterfeit spiritualism. Seances and other foolish probings into the spirit realm prostitute truth. The occult makes religions out of palm reading and psychic phenomena. Those religions are evil and vain, exalting demons as gods and seducing those who participate in worshiping demonic power.

The name "Lucifer" means "light bearer." Because we are taking Lucifer's place before God, we must now be the bearers of God's light. No darkness exists in the Lord because He is Light. We are the sons of Light. As sons of Light, the unified Church will fill every void, regain everything Lucifer has stolen away, and succeed where Lucifer failed. Satan battles us because we are fulfilling the purposes for which God created him! We are creatures of praise who have the power to subdue kingdoms in Jesus' name. Jesus set the example for us by His character and ministry. He was the supreme example of God's creation.

First, Jesus was the extension of His Father. Now we must likewise become an extension of our heavenly Father. He gave us the spiritual gifts—discernment, healing, deliverance, words of wisdom—to extend His ministry in scope and time. We must replace the void in the earth with God's wisdom, love and power which creation lost.

Secondly, Jesus lived a life of praise. Praising the Lord in a worship service is really transitory. Praise must become a lifestyle. Paul wrote, "Rejoice always, pray without ceasing, in everything give thanks; for this is the will of God in Christ Jesus for you" (I Thessalonians 5:16-18).

The peace of God is an inward quality. Our lifestyles should reflect and exemplify peace through praise to God. We must praise Him while we mop the floor or cook a meal. Even if we are in the midst of a "prison" experience, we should give thanks to God. If we lose our jobs because we refuse to compromise Christ-centered ideals, we can still praise God, knowing that He has something better for us. A lifestyle of praise allows no compromise—we show forth His praise, no matter the circumstances, just as Jesus did.

Thirdly, Jesus attacked the religious systems of His day. I agree with the Communist writer Lenin's observation that "religion is an opiate of the people." Religion becomes bondage when it requires us to maintain rigid traditions and legalistic laws. Christianity is a freeing force. Jesus said, "And you shall know the truth, and the truth shall make you free" (John 8:32).

Fourthly, Jesus attacked the economic system of His day. He admonished those who oppressed the poor and confronted the greed of the rich. In God, there is no poverty at all! Jesus came to preach to the poor to tell them how to become rich. We are rich by learning Kingdom principles of sowing and reaping for the Kingdom of God.

Famine in Ethiopia is a spiritual problem. The Communist regime has stripped the people of any motivation they may ever have had. They no longer own property. They have no motivation to sow and reap or make use of their talents. The government has enslaved the people into a poverty mentality. We can send shiploads of food to Ethiopia, and we may prolong life for a matter of hours or even days. But the lasting solution to poverty in Ethiopia or anywhere else is replacing godless government with a government operating by Kingdom principles.

"Liberation theology" throughout Latin America is another reaction to widespread frustration with poverty. Liberation theology holds that poverty has evolved because wealthy capitalists have hoarded all the world's wealth. They claim that the solution to poverty is the redistribution of wealth by violence and revolution. Liberation theologians are basically liberal priests who agree with Marxist ideology toward property holdings. That philosophy kills motivation for progress or creativity. Though the new theology is called "liberation theology," no "liberation" results from it. Those principles of revolution were born out of hell itself.

Fifthly, Jesus attacked the social order. He said, "Why do you consider someone with a beautiful ring on his hand or someone who has a good job to be of more value than someone who is not as financially prosperous?" God causes the rain to fall on the just and the unjust. He is impartial to social status. God gives everyone equal opportunity in terms of productivity and the ability to rise from wherever they are. Evils in our social order are man-made or government-imposed.

We are on earth as extensions of God to finish the work He began. We are the essence of God, His on-going incarnation in the world. The Apostle Peter said that we are "partakers of the divine nature" (II Peter 1:4). If we partake of the divine nature of God as extensions of God, we live as the firstfruit of a new generation of people.

Paul called those who are not partakers of God's nature "children of wrath" (Ephesians 2:3). Disobedient people "walked according to the course of this world, according to the prince of the power of the air . . ." (Ephesians 2:2). They operate by the mind of reason or their own intellects. Jesus spent His ministry teaching harlots and publicans because they were people who knew they were devastated. They were ripe for change and willing to listen.

The Spirit of God within me says that though the devil knows his time is short, he does not truly believe he is already defeated. Satan believes he will rally at the end to overthrow God. We look at events through

the eyes of the prophets who said, "His time is short."
We look at events through God's Word which teaches,
"The devil will be overcome because 'He that is within
us is greater.' " But the devil is telling his cohorts—
those who prostitute and abuse society—"Hey, we're
going to take over! Why should there be any restraints?
Why not be gods unto yourselves? Why respect spiritual authority? Just do what you want to do!"

Karl Marx was a German Jew, born in the early
1800's. He was a man who intently studied religion
until he became frustrated with the church because of
its emphasis on liturgical forms and the architectural
structure of the buildings. Since the church did not
address the plight of the poor and oppressed, Karl
Marx built a new religious system called Marxism out
of his own frustrations. Communism, growing out of
Marx's doctrines, is an atheistic religion. Marx asked,
"If God exists, then where is He?" Tremendous frustration with established religion created a doctrine that
oppresses the world today.

Marxist theologians don't know God; they merely
seek new forms of power. In Ethiopia, where thousands
of people are starving to death, some heads of the
Communist government live in pomp and splendor.
Liberation theology is just a new system of control.
Once it takes control, it will strip people of their God-
given liberties and freedom.

Recently I talked to a young woman from a local
university who is going back into a Communist country to work in television production. She said, "I can't
tell them I got ideas from the Church. I would be

arrested. As long as I say that I got them from an 'educational institution,' I'm allowed to be creative." Many American schools have also been influenced by Communism into rejecting creativity that derives from any source honoring God.

What can we do? God gave me several steps to implement His strategy. God intends for us to withstand the onslaught of the devil in our generation and to aid in accomplishing His work on earth.

First, we must correct our theology. "Theology" is composed of two Greek words that mean "the study of God and things related to Him." We must correct our understanding of God by knowing first that He is a good, loving heavenly Father.

Some pastors tend to think that theological concepts are uniform among Christians. I strongly maintain that one's concept of God determines his actions. If we perceive God to be a loving Father and ourselves as extensions of Him, then we understand and demonstrate His love. If we perceive Him to be an angry tyrant, we reflect that concept of God in our words and deeds. If we believe that every good and perfect gift comes from above, then we respond to that concept of God as a provider, and we act accordingly.

We must also correct our theology of man. Man is not an unworthy "worm." Man was created in the image of Almighty God with the potential of being like Jesus in the world. Man has the potential of demonstrating that Christ-like identity. He must allow the Spirit of God to direct his thoughts and actions toward attaining the full stature of Jesus Christ. A man consumed with becoming like Jesus doesn't sound like a "worm" to me! We must correct our thought patterns about who we are. Success stories which emphasize materialistic gain become tiresome, but sometimes underneath those details is truth—we are made in the image of God with unlimited, tremendous potential.

We must correct our theology about planet earth. The earth must be differentiated from world systems. "Love not the world" does not mean **not** to love the earth that God made. God made no mistakes by ordaining His most prized possession—man—to inhabit the earth. Planet earth is not synonymous with world systems. "God so loved the **world**," not the world's **systems**.

God said, "If My people who are called by My name will humble themselves, and pray and seek My face, and turn from their wicked ways, then I will hear from heaven, and will forgive their sin and heal their land" (II Chronicles 7:14). Healing comes only through activating the principles of our covenant with God—repentance, the Lord's table, tithing and forgiveness. We must maintain our part of the covenant to keep it in effect.

Secondly, we must know our resources. God is our Father, and our resources are God Himself, the Holy Spirit, Jesus Christ and His shed blood. Our weapons are not machetes, machine guns or nuclear missiles.

For the weapons of our warfare are not carnal but mighty in God for pulling down strongholds, casting down arguments and every high thing that exalts itself against the knowledge of God, bringing every thought into captivity to the obedience of Christ, and being ready to punish all disobedience when your obedience is fulfilled. (II Corinthians 10:4-6)

An ounce of love can overcome the atomic bomb! We must learn how to energize a society with God's love. We must understand the value of prayer power. I have observed that **talking** about praying has almost replaced the **act** of praying itself. The time has come to stop having seminars about praying and simply start interceding before God. Prayer should begin and end the day in the house of every saint of God. Prayer should be an integral part of every move we make. Tremendous power is unleashed when we pray.

Power also resides in the spoken word. The tongue has the power of life and death, as well as a mighty creative capacity. One little innuendo from an influential person can destroy the character of a godly man or woman. Words can "make" or "break" the potential for God to work in any situation.

Thirdly, we must have a clear understanding of our assignment.

Then Jesus came and spoke to them, [the disciples] saying, "All authority has been given to Me in heaven and on earth. Go therefore and make disciples of all the nations, baptizing them in the name of the Father and of the Son and of the Holy Spirit, teaching them to observe all things that I have commanded you; and lo, I am with you always, even to the end of the age." Amen. (Matthew 28:18-20)

We are to make disciples of **all** nations. Nations are conglomerates of people, ideologies and influences.

We are now at the end of the age. Jesus has not

abandoned us. He is still "the Captain" of the ship, warring contrary winds. This is the day when we must move in power as never before. Jesus said,

> *The Spirit of the Lord is upon Me, because He has anointed Me to preach the gospel to the poor. He has sent Me to heal the brokenhearted, to preach deliverance to the captives and recovery of sight to the blind, to set at liberty those who are oppressed, to preach the acceptable year of the Lord . . . Today this Scripture is fulfilled in your hearing. (Luke 4:18,19,21)*

In essence Jesus was saying, "The assignment is now complete. I am here. I have come to attack poverty. I have come to set people free from anything that oppresses them personally in government or in society. I have come to bring a new message." That is our assignment today: to implement the message of the Kingdom of God. People who put others into bondage are not identified as God's workmen. In fact, they have never understood God's purposes at all.

Fourthly, we must plan our strategy. Our first priority must be to take on the character of Jesus. Jesus loved. Jesus cared. Jesus touched people and listened to them. We must know and share the power of His love. Jesus said, "By this all will know that you are My disciples, if you have love for one another" (John 13:35). Love is neither a cheap way out nor is it characterized by conformity. Love is an aggressive ability to know who we are in God.

Our seed—our children—are a prime target for corruption. If a seed is corrupted, it grows up deformed or aberrated, if at all. Our children can be disturbed, even destroyed, by mixture and compromise instead of following godly principles of life. We must not allow them to live a life of lies, letting them do, see and hear whatever they choose with no supervision. The most damnable influence in the world today is also potentially the most helpful—visualization of society by television and movies.

We must infiltrate the media through Christian newspaper writers and editors who openly acknowledge God, and news commentators who speak with an understanding of God's Word. If we are going to change our society, we must learn how to capture public attention. We must make movies that will surpass the movies produced in Hollywood.

A society which condones the use of drugs, alcohol and pornography creates a generation that will eventually be unable to think with any sense of order. Our strategy must be an aggressive attack against current standards of immorality. We must reclaim the arts, drama, theater, dance—every good and perfect gift which originated with God. The Church will undergo many battles for the stands that we take. We already experience opposition because we dance in the church—but we won't quit! We are simply going to continue to dance in a way that pleases God. We will dress and move properly, and dance to the glory of the Lord.

We must know the meaning and power of the blood covenant. When we are in covenant with God, we can use the name of Jesus Christ to defeat the devil. We can say, "Devil, in the name of Jesus, you get out of here!

Satan, in the name of Jesus, you have no authority here!" This proclamation is no "guessing game"! It will work! It will work anywhere—Ethiopia, Latin America or Atlanta, Georgia!

The Kingdom of God was Jesus' main emphasis during His earthly ministry. For the forty days after His resurrection, He preached only the Kingdom. Before He ascended to His Father, the apostles asked Him, "Will You now restore the Kingdom to Israel?" His answer to them implied, "You didn't hear a thing I said! I'm not trying to rebuild Solomon's or David's kingdoms. Receive the Holy Spirit! Go out and preach the Kingdom of God to the whole world—Jerusalem, Judea, Samaria, the uttermost parts of the earth. I will give you the power to be My witnesses."

Finally, we must visualize the results of our strategy. We need to be dreamers. We won't be popular; dreamers never are. We may even be hated and persecuted. The Kingdom of God is within, so we must visualize it. Attacks against ministries of men like Robert Schuller, Pastor Cho and me are made because we visualize results. We dream. Those who attack us say that visualization is not of God. For every evil thing, a good counterpart exists. The Bible speaks of a wicked imagination; its counterpart is a godly imagination. Everything we ever accomplish for God is first conceived in our minds. Visualize the Kingdom!

They shall not hurt nor destroy in all My holy mountain, for the earth shall be full of the knowledge of the Lord as the waters cover the sea. (Isaiah 11:9)

Arise, shine; for your light has come! And the glory of the Lord is risen upon you. For behold, the darkness shall cover the earth, and deep darkness the people; but the Lord will arise over you, and His glory will be seen upon you. The Gentiles shall come to your light, and kings to the brightness of your rising. (Isaiah 60:1-3)

When the earth understands the knowledge of the Lord, and God speaks to people with Daniel and Joseph spirits, politicians will run for public office only after seeking direction from God's prophets.

The "great mountain" that will fill the whole earth (Daniel 2:35) is the Kingdom of God. All the kingdoms of the earth will bow before it. "The kingdoms of this world have become the kingdoms of our Lord and of His Christ, and He shall reign forever and ever!" (Revelation 11:15).

The wicked plots against the just, and gnashes at him with his teeth. The Lord laughs at him, for He sees that his day is coming . . . For the arms of the wicked shall be broken, but the Lord upholds the righteous. The Lord knows the days of the upright, and their inheritance shall be forever . . . But the wicked shall perish . . . For those who are blessed by Him shall inherit the earth, but those who are cursed by Him shall be cut off. The steps of a good man are ordered by the Lord, and He delights in his way. Though he fall, he shall not be utterly cast down; for the Lord upholds him with His hand. I have been young, and now am old; yet I have not seen the righteous forsaken, nor His descendants begging bread. He is ever merciful, and lends; and His descendants are blessed . . . But the descendants of the wicked shall be cut off. The righteous shall inherit the land, and dwell in it forever . . . The wicked watches the righteous, and seeks to slay him . . . And He shall exalt you to inherit the land; when the wicked are cut off, you shall see it . . . Yet he passed away, and behold, he was no more . . .(Psalm 37:12-36)

The future of the wicked is dark, but the future of God's children is bright. The hour has come for the Church to enter into covenant with God to help Him complete His work on planet earth. Our assignment is clear. God has given us the Holy Spirit and empowered us to do His work. Now the challenge to us is moving ahead boldly in the power of God to accomplish the greatest task ever given to mankind—the establishment of the Kingdom of God on earth!

ABOUT THE AUTHOR

Bishop Earl Paulk is senior pastor of Chapel Hill Harvester Church located in Atlanta, Georgia. Chapel Hill Harvester Church has twenty full-time pastors serving a local parish of over ten thousand people with thousands more receiving ministry by television and outreach ministries.

Bishop Paulk grew up in a classical Pentecostal family as the son of Earl P. Paulk Sr., a former assistant general overseer of the Church of God. His grandfather, Elisha Paulk, was a Freewill Baptist preacher.

Personal and educational exposure have given Bishop Paulk an ecumenical understanding enjoyed by few church leaders in the world today. He earned a Bachelor of Arts degree from Furman University which is a Baptist institution and a Master's of Divinity degree from Candler School of Theology which is a Methodist seminary.

Earl Paulk was named to the office of Bishop in the International Communion of Charismatic Churches in 1982. He assumes oversight of many churches, directly and indirectly influenced by the ministry of Chapel Hill Harvester Church. The church hosts an annual Pastors' Conference in which leaders from local churches across the nation absorb anointed teaching, observe ministry demonstration and have the opportunity for personal dialogue on the major concerns confronting the Church today.

Under Bishop Paulk's leadership, Chapel Hill Harvester Church has become a successful working prototype of a true Kingdom Church. The foundation of the church is Kingdom principles applied to the biblical concept of a City of Refuge.

The church ministries include a home for unwed mothers; a licensed child placement agency; ministry to those chemically addicted and their families; a ministry to those wishing to come out of the homosexual community; outreach programs to nursing homes, prisons, and homebound individuals; Alpha, one of the most widely acclaimed youth ministries in the nation; and many other ministries designed to meet the needs of the Body of Christ.

Television outreach through the Harvester Television Network is the "Earl Paulk" program seen weekly on P.T.L. Satellite Network, Trinity Broadcasting Network, Rock Network and numerous other television outlets nationwide. Bishop Paulk is frequently a guest on major television and radio interview programs, discussing his books and issues which focus on the Kingdom message.

Other books by K-Dimension Publishers

The Divine Runner	*Earl Paulk*
The Wounded Body of Christ	*Earl Paulk*
Ultimate Kingdom	*Earl Paulk*
Satan Unmasked	*Earl Paulk*
Sex Is God's Idea	*Earl Paulk*
Held In The Heavens Until . . .	*Earl Paulk*
To Whom Is God Betrothed?	*Earl Paulk*
The Provoker	*Tricia Weeks*
My All-Sufficient One	*Sharon Price*

For further information please contact—

P.O. Box 7300 • Atlanta, GA 30357

Chapel Hill Harvester Church
Harvest Time
P.O. Box 371289
Decatur, Georgia 30037

Chapel Hill Harvester Church publishes a monthly newsletter, *Harvest Time*, which is available by subscription for $10.00 per year.

If you would like to subscribe to *Harvest Time*, send the following form or a facsimile, along with your payment, to:

Chapel Hill Harvester Church
Harvest Time
P.O. Box 371289
Decatur, Georgia 30037

Name _____

Address _____

City _____ State _____

Zip Code _____ Phone (_____)_____
                           Area Code   Number

Chapel Hill Harvester Church
Harvest Time
P.O. Box 371250
Decatur, Georgia 30037

Chapel Hill Harvester Church publishes
a monthly newsletter, Harvest Time, which
is available by subscription for $10.00 per
year.

If you would like to subscribe to Harvest
Time, send the following form on a duplicate
along with your payment to:

Chapel Hill Harvester Church
Harvest Time
P.O. Box 371250
Decatur, Georgia

Name _____

Address _____

City _____ State _____

Zip Code _____ Phone _____
                    Area Code   Number